Life Is...

Ray Rouse

xulon PRESS

～o～

This book is dedicated to the caregivers of the world-those people who graciously give of their time to care for parents, grandparents, children, siblings, grandchildren, and friends. Without their helpfulness, life would not be worth living for masses of us. God bless them all.

Acknowledgements

∞o∞

I would like to thank all those people who had stories to tell and allowed me to share them with my readers; you will meet them as you progress through the book.

I also appreciate the guidance afforded me by Charles R. Brown, Faye G. Phillips, Kenneth R. Rouse, Marilyn Rouse, and Eleanor P. Smith.

The help I received from employees of Kinston-Lenoir County Library is also appreciated, as was that from John Watson.

And I commend Debbie Davis, student at the local Lenoir Community College, for the masterful job she performed in typing the manuscript. This was her first venture and she did well.

Front cover and other art designed by Eddie Cox, Kinston, NC.

Contents

ᵛᵛᵛ

INTRO

⌇⌇

Many years ago there was a popular song that had these words in it: "Life is just a bowl of cherries", indicating life is always wonderful.

Wouldn't it be great if this were really true? What if we really could cruise through life without sickness, financial problems, grief or heartache? I can't believe this has ever occurred in the life of a single adult in this world. That type of life is yet to come-in another world-at another time. We can take heart, however; this has been promised us through Holy Scriptures, until then, we do the best we can.

My first book, "They Didn't Bring Ice on Sunday", was self-published and put on the market in May 2002. It was an autobiography which I referred to as a "fun" book. I had fun writing it and fun marketing it. It covered my life from birth through the Great Depression and into the year 2001.

The book was sprinkled with humor and dotted with tragedy. I wanted to make readers laugh and make them cry in the same publication. Judging from the many comments I was the beneficiary of, I must have succeeded in that one goal, at least.

I touched on economic conditions in our area of Eastern North Carolina during the 1920s and 1930s, when my older brothers worked 10 and 12-hour days for daily pay of 35 to 50 cents, which was not uncommon in that era. This fact brought responses from numerous people who had lived in similar circumstances.

Not long after the book was offered for sale, a reader called and related to me his family's financial situation during that same period. It seems that his father was employed by the City of Kinston as operator of a street sweeper. His salary was ten dollars per week, which wasn't a bad deal, but there was a "kicker" to it. In order to get paid, he had to go to the court house on Saturdays and wait for taxpayers to come in and pay their property taxes-from which source his salary was paid. There were some weeks when the city did not collect enough to pay him, resulting in a carryover to the next week.

The book title also elicited many comments from elderly readers who remembered those times. The horse-drawn ice wagon would come by their houses Monday through Saturday at which time they would run to the wagon and scoop up ice slivers while the ice man was carrying ice inside the homes. And that ritual wasn't limited to our part of the country-it occurred all across the forty-eight states.

Each reader seemed to have a tale to share about his or her experiences with the ice man.

It wasn't a really big problem delivering the product in our small town, since practically all deliveries were ground floor. Can you imagine, however, what problems could occur in big cities like New York or Chicago, where apartment buildings were multi-storied?

Place yourself in the shoes of an ice man who has a customer on the eighth floor (no elevator) who gave you a standing order for a 50 pound piece to be delivered twice weekly. It's Monday morning and you're a little hung over from slurping a few too many suds over the weekend, but you've got this delivery to make. You separate a 50 pound piece from the block, sink tongs into it and throw it onto your back, which is protected by a leather pad. You proceed to stomp up eight flights of steps. When you reach your destination you're bushed-perspiration from an overworked body blending with ice drippings and gradually soaking everything from your waist down. You feel terrible and look like you've just been pulled from the Hudson.

On top of that, you're tired of leaning forward to prevent yourself from being pulled backward and falling back down the eight flights.

After bruising your knuckles by knocking on your customers' door for about five minutes, it's opened by a very attractive young lady, combing her hair. She's dressed to kill and you're looking like a dog.

"Oh, Jim, it's you. I'm sorry to cause you all this trouble, but we're leaving on vacation today and we won't need any ice this week. Sam asked me to call you, but I forgot."

Neither did I anticipate another type of feedback from the book's readers. For instance, I never knew that so many people had, at one time or another, lived on Tower Hill Road, where I had lived at age five. I was even told by one lady that her family had moved into that very house immediately after we vacated it in 1929.

That was the location at which I had played underneath the house on rainy days and tried to lure "doodlebugs" out of their holes with saliva soaked sticks. I did not dwell on the subject at the time-I just stuck it in the narrative as an insignificant anecdote.

About two or three weeks after my first book signing, I received correspondence from a reader that included, not only a history of the bug, but a copy of a song entitled "The Doodlebug Song". It was written by C.E. Moody over seventy-five years ago.

The sender's name was Etta Oliver, who is married to Elwood Oliver, a minister of the gospel, with whom I have something in common. He and I were drafted into the U.S. Army on the same day, January 28, 1943. We also rode the same troop train from Fort Bragg, NC, to California.

Etta informed me she had found this bit of bug trivia in an old recipe book at her home. I hope I took time to call her and thank her for her kindness. If I did not: "Thanks Etta".

For the benefit of "Ice"-and new readers, following is the "Bug" history, as well as the song's words:

The Doodlebug Song
By C.E. Moody

When I was a kid this is what I did,

Just to pass the time away. I'd look all around until I

found, A doodle hole then I'd say.

Chorus

Hey doodle doodle hop up bug,

Hey doodle doodle hop up bug,

That Doodle bug hop up and jump all around,

Then doodle back in the ground.

What a pleasure to me, it was to see

That doodle coming out.

I'd squat right down and watch that clown

Twist his head about.

Chorus

I don't know why, to a doodle I'd lie

But this is what I'd say,

"Your house is a fire, your children are cryin'

You better come out this way!"

Chorus

DOODLEBUGS

The Doodlebug Song was recorded in 1928 by a group called the Georgia Yellowhammers. The doodlebug is the larval stage of a small insect known in the books as an antlion. It inhabits dry sandy areas where it constructs funnel-shaped pit traps to catch ants and other insects. Buried in the sand at the bottom of the funnel, the doodlebug waits and when an unfortunate insect stumbles into its funnel, the doodlebug starts twisting its head about creating a miniature landslide. The victim, unable to get any traction on the sides of the funnel, eventually slides to the bottom of the pit into the waiting sickle-like jaws of the antlion to be pulled under the sand and devoured. It is not always easy to find a doodlebug in its pit because these critters remain motionless when disturbed and when dug up, they are covered with a layer of sand or dust and are easily overlooked. The best way to see a doodlebug in action is to first locate one of the pits in a dry sandy place. Then gently touch the sides of the funnel with a tiny twig or stiff blade of grass imitating an ant scurrying up the sides and watch the doodlebug do a "jitterbug" and flail its jaws all about. Or better yet, try it with a live ant. A hungry doodlebug will appreciate the snack.

With a little practice, you can often get the doodlebug to move about by putting your mouth close to the doodlebug's pit and singing, "Hey doodle, doodle, hop up bug," several times. This is an old tradition in doodlebug country practiced by many generations of children. If that doesn't work, you can "lie" to the doodlebug and tell it that its house is on fire and its children are crying. Of course the doodlebug is really just a youngster itself and has no children. It will spin a cocoon of silk and sand to late emerge as an adult which looks something like a delicate dragonfly.

A number of readers have asked me if I was going to write another book. My answer in each instance was, "No, I lived only one life and it's all in that book." Well, we all have the prerogative to change our minds.

After the book reached local book store shelves I was invited to appear on local TV programs, where the same question was asked by the interviewers: "Ray, why did you write this book?" A simple enough question-right? Well, I didn't have a simple answer. I wasn't sure exactly why I had done it. I hadn't been inspired by any partic-ular person or event.

When I returned home one day after a round of golf, I sat down at one of the round tables on our porch, found a pen and pad and began writing. Annie, my wife, came out and asked me what I was doing. "I'm going to see if I can possibly write a manuscript that might be worth reading". "What's it about?" "It's about my life, an autobiography." Unenthusiastically-"Well, good luck."

Have you ever wanted to try something just to see if you could do it? I think that was my basic reason for attempting it, but after I really got into it, I realized I was having fun-so I just kept on writing. After all, I was simply relating on paper some events that had occurred in my life and those of my family. I began with my birth in 1924, which I recalled vividly, and ended with events occurring 2001-when I ended the narrative.

Since I had handwritten it, I needed to find someone to type it, which I did. I then prevailed upon a friend to look it over and point out my mistakes, which he did. At that point I still did not know what I would do with the completed manuscript. I began contacting local printing shops in hope of finding one which could turn the "thing" into a book. No luck. In our city of about 23,000 people I could find no one here to do the job. One printer, however, referred me to a print firm in a nearby city which could do the job for a price.

Having been a financially astute person all my life, I didn't especially want a pleasant experience turn into an unpleasant one by having a lot of books printed that might not sell. Annie wasn't sure any of them would sell, except to family members.

I first presented my project to a small group of men at a church meeting and when I left there I had orders for about 20 books. I felt like then I would be safe in having 100 books printed.

You know, once in a while even morons come up with a bright idea. It was my turn. From high school reunions I had accumulated addresses of classmates from my class of 1942. Maybe they would like a book. I made telephone calls to all parts of our country and almost everyone ordered a copy. I increased my book order to 150, then to 200, and then to 300. Annie said, "That's all." "No, I believe I can get rid of 350." That became my number.

At that point I approached the owner of the local "Book Depot", who agreed to put my books on her shelves when I picked them up from the printer.

She set up a book signing date-after which I contacted a representative of our local newspaper, to whom I divulged my venture and gave the date of the book signing.

Then I was blessed with a little luck, something we can all use once in a while. Just a couple of days before the Kinston Free Press article was to appear, a delay in the book printing occurred, which meant the book signing date had to be changed-in a hurry! The book store owner was able to change her schedule and delay the signing period. I immediately contacted the newspaper representative who advised me their article was to appear in the next day's edition, but there was time for them to make the correction. She was extremely cooperative and made the last minute change, but somewhere along the line communications broke down, resulting in two different dates being shown for the book signing. You might ask, "How could that be lucky?" Well, when the error was caught, the newspaper's next day edition was plastered with correction notices in three or four locations of the paper. Great advertising! Some friends even asked me if I had financial interest in the organization.

I guess the most fun of the entire episode was derived from the marketing of the book. At book signings I renewed old acquaintances and made new ones. Many of them recalled the "old days", when most people struggled to earn enough money to put food on the tables and clothes on their backs.

Selling of the books went well and within a relatively short time the 350 copies were gone. I then thought I was out of the book business, but I was being contacted by a few people who wanted books. Ignoring objections from Annie, I ordered another 100 books. At a second book signing at "Book Depot" a few months later they were all sold except 13. My children advised me not to sell the remainder, saying sometime in the future some special friends would appear and ask for a book. That happened and the books disappeared. They are now things of a memorable past.

Unlike "Ice", I couldn't put this book in the category of "fun books"-so how would I describe it-what really is its subject? You might also ask me how I came up with the title.

"They Didn't Bring Ice On Sunday" turned out to be the perfect title for the other book. It just came out of the blue early on and I was never tempted to change it.

I did, however, have a problem deciding on a title for the one you are reading. Simply "Life" would have been an appropriate title, because I deal with several aspects of life, but I would have run into trouble with infringement of copyright laws due to a magazine by the same name.

By simply reading the title of this book you can imagine the connotations that could be arrived at from a title such as <u>Life is...</u>. What intrigued me about the title is that the possibilities of subjects to write about are endless.

When a human is born that person immediately enters the process of dying. The death thing can occur immediately after birth, or it could take a hundred years, or more, for life to end. During that period we encounter innumerable periods of sorrow, joy, frustrations, pains, horrors, disbelief, exhilaration, fatigue, fear, contentment and countless other emotions.

You will encounter all these within the pages of this book. They are all a part of life. I suspect all of us have, at some time or another come face to face with all these facets of life.

"Ice" was simple to write, since it is an autobiography. All I had to do was to write about the highlights of my life and make them as interesting as possible.

I soon discovered it's another whole ball game when you begin writing about the lives of others. And that's what <u>Life is...</u> entails.

I discovered early on that one doesn't have to stray far from home in order to uncover many intriguing life situations, so I began gathering fodder for my manuscript right here in the City of Kinston, NC. I then branched out as needed in order to achieve a broader scope of life's meaning.

I cover a real life experience dating back to 1910, which revolves around a lady who is still living, and as of this writing, is still very active with a story to tell.

You will also travel side by side with a retired local physician as he leads you through twenty years of hellish mental illness while still carrying on a medical practice for much of that time.

Then you will meet a courageous lady who suffered through a double tragedy after retirement-but pulled herself up by the boot straps and continued a meaningful existence. It's here you will need to keep a kerchief handy when you read about how a young lady chooses to laud the one person in life who has meant more to her than anyone else. And this is done just days before she knows she faces death.

I will also, introduce you to a most wonderful lady, one who possibly is endowed with more talent than anyone I personally know. She has had more than her share of life's misfortunes, including disability from one of our rarest diseases. Despite this, she says she is happier now than at any time in her life.

And who of us have gone through life without witnessing what we consider a miracle?

You will marvel at some real life ones experienced by some of the book's characters — and others — which lead us to believe there is a higher power who steps up and intervenes in our lives occasionally.

You will gasp at some of the hardships the human body can endure when a small group of men escape a Russian prison camp in Siberia and walk for twelve months through every conceivable climate to gain freedom.

I explore many activities of everyday life and delve into a lot of "whys" and "wherefores". That's why I titled the book what I did.

If you were to come up with a list of different sides of life, I'm sure they would differ from mine. I hope you enjoy reading my list.

Before venturing into "Life is...", I would like to digress and tell about a couple of events that have occurred in my life since I marketed "Ice". You probably will not consider them as significant as I do.

First of all, I've had another hole-in-one on the local golf course. It was on hole #5, a short one of only 110 yards, but an ace is an ace is an ace. I swung a 13 wood perfectly—it took one bounce and disappeared.

The other significant event occurred April 25, 2004. That was my eightieth birthday.

We had recently attended several such events, which had led me to wonder why the eightieth was so special to so many people. Neither Annie nor I had put any special significance on any other birthday. Have any of you old folks considered why so much emphasis seems to have been placed on this one?

Couldn't it be because in all likelihood, it would be the last decade we would have the privilege of ushering in? Maybe. For me, it also meant a couple of other things. For one-it represented the last time I would be able to secure an unrestricted drivers license renewal. This time I barely passed the sight portion of the test, due to a lot of help from a very nice agent.

Also, it would probably be the last time I would purchase a new car. When we buy a new one we usually drive it for ten years and at age 90 I probably won't even be driving a car-that is, if I'm still living.

Whatever the significance, I had a celebration of sorts. Annie's five siblings and spouses were there; my brother and his wife from Greenville drove over; my sister-in-law from Goldsboro was in attendance; and our son from Asheville was here. When you get that many relatives together and they are all amicable, a good time can be had by all.

The most important thing to do on such occasions is to feed the crowd well-and that we did. It was a southern style layout featuring barbecue chicken and barbecue pork, along with sweet potatoes, butter beans, corn and all that other stuff that's so palatable down south.

My 86-year-old, sometimes hard to please brother, even complimented us on the meal. He especially liked the barbecue pork, of which he had more than one serving.

Our little outing was quite enjoyable, as were the other three we had recently attended. Yes, number 80 is somehow special.

In finishing up this "Intro", let me say one more thing.

I ended "Ice" by describing the ritual of receiving 39 sessions of radiation in order to cure me of prostate cancer.

In the consultation with the physician prior to the sessions, he promised to kill the cancer, but he also warned me that later in life the treatment I was about to undergo would cause another cancer of some type—possibly 14 or 15 years later.

Well, he apparently killed that big-C because it has now been more than five years since those treatments were begun. This means I have used up that many of the good years he hoped I would have.

Except for having one of the side effects that I was warned might occur, I have felt good for these five years. I have been able to continue the physical activities I enjoyed prior to treatment. All seems to be well.

Good reading!

LIFE IS…

Ray Rouse

EVERYBODY HAS A STORY TO TELL

CHAPTER ONE
LIFE IS — A SIGN

I t was a typical November day in Eastern North Carolina as the diver dressed in typical regalia and slipped into the waters of the Neuse River. The water was cool, but not yet cold. Weather in the area doesn't usually turn cold until December, as a rule.

The Neuse is not a large river when compared to the country's major water arteries. It has a beginning in the Piedmont portion of North Carolina and has a total length of just under 200 miles. It empties into the Pamlico Sound, below the City of New Bern, at which point it becomes much wider and deeper. Before reaching New Bern it passes in close proximity to the cities of Durham, Raleigh, Smithfield, Goldsboro, and Kinston.

One of the river's claims to historical fame lies in the fact that one of the Confederate Navy's ironclad warships of the Civil War was constructed on its banks near the village of Seven Springs in

1865 and then floated down to Kinston, 18 miles downstream. Due to low water in the Kinston area, the boat, Ram Neuse, lodged on a sandbar and was later scuttled by the crew to prevent it from being of any benefit to Northern forces.

The point at which the divers entered the water-close to the village of Fort Barnwell-was fairly narrow.

The purpose of the water search was to find the body of a fisherman who had reportedly drowned in the immediate area.

Not too long after entering the murky waters of the Neuse, one of the divers spotted an object resting on the bottom of the river some distance away. As the diver moved closer he realized it couldn't be a human body-it was too big. It was a minivan-and it was occupied!

No-the divers had not found what they had been looking for, but had they just solved a mystery that had plagued the sheriff departments of Lenoir and Craven counties for almost a year? Would an inexplicable event that occurred in December 2004 now become explicable?

*   *   *

Have you ever considered what an important part signs play in our everyday lives? They are placed on our highways and byways to protect us from each other. These machines called vehicles can become deadly weapons in our hands when we don't obey traffic signs. This can also happen, when for some reason, we fail to see a sign due to oversight.

I would refer to these type signs as directional ones. They tell us where to go and how to get there. The most obvious ones, of course, are on this great interstate highway system we have-and I mean it's truly great. A person can conceivably drive from our east coast to the west coast without hitting a traffic light. The same applies to driving from Maine to Florida.

On all those routes are huge signs telling us what exit to take in order to reach our destination and how far away it is. In most areas those signs are easy to follow, but in huge metropolitan areas they can be so plentiful and close together that we need to be on our P's and Q's in order not to miss any.

On non-interstates we have smaller ones, usually on the shoulders, that advise us of curves in the road, no passing and myriad other advisories-including detour signs. These are usually erected when road construction is underway. They show us what alternate road to take to avoid construction activities that could endanger lives. We have to be careful not to miss a single directional sign on the detour in order to get back on the primary road. If we fail to do that it can mean danger-real danger.

This fact was brought to light in our Kinston, North Carolina area on that fateful day in December 2004.

A fifty-eight year old grandmother and her sixteen year old granddaughter were victims of a tragic accident involving a detour incident.

The two left Kinston in the wee hours of the morning on December 7. They had told relatives they were going to visit relatives in Virginia, but were first going to deliver some flowers to a friend who lived some miles east of Kinston on Hwy 55. They never reached their destination. They simply disappeared.

Sometime before daylight the grandmother's estranged husband received a cell phone call from her, which was apparently a call for help. He said his wife screamed and said she was drowning, but that was all she said. No mention of her location.

Records of the cellular phone company showed that the call was made either from Lenoir County or from some place close by.

The search was on. Except for the phone call, there was no evidence to go on, despite many calls from interested parties. Authorities used every type of equipment they had at their disposal in their search for the two women. They used sonar-equipped boats, dogs, helicopters, and ATV's without success. Roads from Kinston to Virginia were searched and waters in the phone area were dragged-all without a favorable result.

It was as if the two people simply disappeared from the face of the earth. What had happened? All sorts of theories began surfacing. Had they conveniently gone into hiding deliberately? If so, why couldn't the vehicle be found? Alerts had been put out in other states. Was it possible the two had been victims of foul play? Maybe the grandmother had become disoriented and simply got lost.

Isn't it strange how, at times, one thing can lead to another? This mystery, unlike that of Jimmy Hoffa-which has lasted for decades-would not go unsolved forever.

When this professional diver, who had also made such water searches months before vainly looking for the two women, got close enough to identify the personalized license plate, GAIL-RN, he realized he had stumbled onto the van involved in the incident. He then saw that the van contained two bodies-both females. When the vehicle was retrieved the two bodies were verified to be those of the grandmother and grandchild.

What had happened? What had caused this horrible incident to occur? There is no way to be absolutely certain of the events that had led to the deaths, but authorities, after piecing together every detail, came up with a probable scenario.

The twosome left Kinston and drove east on Hwy 55. After driving some distance they came upon road construction which necessitated a detour sign being placed there. The driver left 55 and took the designated road. At some point on that road she missed seeing another sign directing them back to the highway. How did she fail to see the sign? Well, she could have been assisting her grand-daughter in some way, causing her attention to be diverted from the road-or maybe darkness was the cause. Instead of turning, she continued straight onto a secondary road known as Turkey Quarter Landing Road, a route taken regularly by fishermen to reach the landing from which to launch their boats. In the darkness she had no way of knowing she was approaching the river-and sure death. When the van hit the water she had no time to do anything but make that one very abbreviated phone call to her husband.

Two deaths-due to the fact a sign that had been placed there to assist the drivers-had not been seen.

Just suppose we had no signs. At one time we didn't. Of course cave men had no need for them, you know. They had no highways, no restaurants, no motels and *no restrooms*. Nowadays, all these places and others require signs.

When we old folks enter a building and plan to remain there for any length of time, the first thing we look for is a sign over some door that says "restrooms". For old geezers who've had prostate cancer and mature ladies needing tummy tucks, this is the most reas-suring sign they hope to see.

For travelers, highway signs promoting eateries are welcome sights about meal time, after driving for hours without food. The same applies for hotels and motels.

This fact was brought to light for our son, Mike and me in 1985 when we were taking a whirlwind, two week tour of Europe.

One of the first things we became aware of was the scarcity of places to find a good night's rest, unless we stopped moving well before nightfall. One day stands out in my mind as being very troublesome.

We had no itinerary and were playing everything by ear, but we did possess a map of Europe. On this particular day we were a little late leaving Avignon, France, which made arriving at the French Riviera a little late also.

Not wanting to spend the night there, we gassed up and headed north. There were lots of little cars blowing horns and running into each other in the city, plus the fact we made a wrong turn, that caused us to be further delayed. Night befell us in the middle of nowhere. We headed for Aosta, Italy. After driving for some time and before reaching the city-we beheld a most welcome sign beside the highway: "Motel City ahead". What joy! Not only did it promise a place to rid ourselves of fatigue, we could probably have a choice of rooms, plus a restaurant meal. How many motels would be located in the "City"? Would there be four, five, or more? Would we begin our sumptuous evening meal with a bottle of wine-compliments of the establishment? All of these questions would be answered shortly.

Soon we rounded a curve, and sure enough we saw bright lights. There they were-TWO motels. Small city. Not to worry though, all we wanted was one room in one motel. We lifted our bags from the rented Fiesta and entered the motel. "Sorry sir, we are filled up. You might try the one next door." Motel #2: "Sorry sir, we have no vacancy." "Do you know where we might find lodging for the night?" "Why don't you drive to Aosta and look for the Ambassador Hotel? They might have a vacancy."

We found the place about 10:00 p.m. When we entered and made our inquiry we were told they did have one vacant room-for five people! Regardless of the cost, we had to have a room. Both of us were about shot. We told him there would be only two of us and we were pleasantly surprised when the night manager told us we could have the room at the two people rate. Good deal! Maybe he figured that at 10:00 p.m. two tourists in house were better then five on the highway.

How about food? Was there any available at this time of night? The manager advised us their restaurant was closed, but then told us he would have their chef provide us with some sliced ham, bread, and cantaloupe, which we welcomed with gratitude-and was more delicious than the "Nabs" and bottled water we had in the car.

The hotel was old, but elegant. The room was huge with enough room for us to ramble around. After figuring out how to flush the john and turn on the shower, we hit the sack and died for about eight hours. Total cost for the room, evening snack and breakfast was $47.06.

Even though the road sign hadn't immediately afforded us the result we desired, it did play an important part in helping us acquire board and lodging.

In traveling, you occasionally come across a unique sign, the only one of its kind. On our train ride from London to Dover I had picked up a flyer that plugged the Royal St. George's Golf Club which was located in a town called Sandwich. Mike and I had played the Old Course in St. Andrews, Scotland, prior to crossing the Channel to enter France, and I was intrigued by the flyer extolling the course in Sandwich. So, the day before crossing the Channel to get back to England, I called the people at Royal St. George's to determine if we could play their course the next day. The person I conversed with was extremely cordial and he let me know we would be welcome as visiting golfers. He then invited us to have lunch with some members in their club house. I told him neither Mike nor I had proper attire to participate in activities in somewhat formal surroundings. He assured me they had proper jackets in the club house which they would be glad to lend us. I graciously thanked him, but I begged off by saying we wouldn't have time to do anything other then play a fast round. What nice people.

Mike decided not to play, so he acted as caddy. The golf course, which is world class, is located beside the English Channel. It was September and the weather was perfect. The course was a joy to play. The year after we played it, the world famous British Open was held there.

The town of Sandwich has existed for centuries and is quite a tourist attraction. It's also home to a research and development center owned by Pfizer, the renowned pharmaceutical company, and is the site where Viagra was discovered.

The town is also noted as the location of a most unique sign. A village named Ham is located in the vicinity of Sandwich and not too far away is a road sign which shows the name of both places on the same signboard. The word "Ham" is on top and "Sandwich" is below it. It is reported that the sign is replaced occasionally due to its theft. By the way, if you're interested in how the town obtained its name-it is alleged that one of the early Earls of the town (no pun intended) invented the original item that is so popular around the world as a favorite snack.

*   *   *

Back in 1951 Annie and I were helped greatly by a number of signs that lined the highways between Kinston and California. That was the time she and I wrapped weekends around the two-week vacations and made our first trip to California-to see Hollywood, which was about as far as we could go without entering the Pacific. Time was of the essence, inasmuch as there were no interstates at the time, meaning we had to drive straight through the entire major cities between here and there.

We drove to Selma, Alabama, the first day. Our plan for the second day was to drive to Dallas and spend the night. All motel signs along the way said "no vacancy", so we kept going until we reached Fort Worth, where we finally saw a neon sign that said "vacancy". What welcome words. We were bushed! We went inside, extracted travelers checks from billfold and paid $3.50 for the night's lodging and hit the sack.

Yes, signs can be very helpful and most welcome on occasions.

And then there are signs of warning, a few of which we've also run across.

On our way across Texas, in remote areas there were small restrooms located on shoulders of the road. In those days there were long stretches of road on which you saw no buildings-and those little 8 x 10 structures were a delight to see. One had to be cautious before entering, however. Posted near the entrance was usually a short sign containing the following words: "beware of rattlesnakes".

Later in life, specifically 1987, we visited the Little Bighorn Battlefield in Crow Agency, Montana, where General George Custer and his brigade were wiped out. There was a path leading through an open field down to the spots where bodies of the soldiers were found after the battle. There was a marker where each one had fallen-all white except one black one which represented the location where Custer was found. I took the path that led down to that spot, but not before looking at the little sign at the path's entrance that had the same words of advice: "beware of rattlesnakes".

And how many times have I read western novels and seen "cowboy shows" that depicted gold miners or cowboys straggling across a desert, desperate for water? They would see an oasis area containing a pond. When reaching it they would start to kneel in order to gulp that lifesaving liquid and they would spot a small sign saying: "poison water". Yes, there are many danger signs to help protect us.

I also recall a warning sign I ran across while on the European trip with Mike. After crossing the English Channel by ferry, we spent the night in Calais and the next day we drove to Omaha Beach, where my army division landed on July 6, 1944. While there, we visited Point-du-Hoc, just a short distance away. It was there where 250 rangers ascended a steep cliff at dawn and by noon there were only 90 survivors. The area had been left in its original state-which resulted in signs being placed in certain areas which read: "Danger-Mines". Another example of warning signs.

*　　*　　*

Many years ago I saw a newspaper cartoon that impressed me greatly. It depicted a huge desolate area in the middle of nowhere. No buildings, no trees. Nothing but a great expanse of sandy soil with little vegetation, except for three items: A highway crossroads, a traffic light with the red glowing and a lone motorist waiting for the red to turn green. The light must have been suspended on sky hooks. The cartoonist had to have been a great humorist in order to paint this scene of a driver waiting for the green in an area seemingly void of vehicular traffic-or any other sign of life.

Do you suppose you could find *anybody* who would be conscientious enough to obey traffic signs to that extent?

Just a stones throw from my house is one of those "all way" stop signs that we are seeing more and more frequently at intersections. One day I decided to spend a quarter hour observing this particular spot to see first hand just how many people would obey the stop sign. The intersection is not an especially busy one. Following is an eye witness account of my experiment.

The first car is coming north on Greenbriar. It is an oldie-doesn't look too good. It holds two male occupants. They don't look so hot either. They stop completely. I'm surprised, but wait, the passenger side door is opening. Is the guy gonna jump out? Is he a possessor of cocaine who sees a cop approaching from the rear? The door opens fully, but then is shut. Oh well, the door must have been ajar and the driver stopped in order for the passenger to safely close it. I let my suspicious mind run amuck.

There comes a covey of three SUV's. They are so close to each other that it's almost a tailgating situation. All three drivers do the same thing. They hit the brakes and slow down considerably-some refer to that procedure as the "California Roll".

Approaching from the south is a white, shining, sports coupe driven by a very nice looking, sweet young thing. She appears to be having happy thoughts. Probably thinking about that boyfriend whom she's been trying to meet for weeks-and who called her this a.m. for a date. She's thinking about that, or something else, because she hardly touches the brake, just enough to make some semblance of slowing down. No harm done though. I suspect if I were a young unmarried cop I would feel compelled to stop her and at least check her driver's license.

Next comes a red, white, and blue panel truck. The young man driving, in addition to being a patriotic soul, must also be a careful driver. He brings his vehicle to a standstill. Very impressive.

Here comes a young, attractive lady heading south in a new SUV, with a cell phone stuck to her ear. Surprisingly, she comes up to a complete stop. She throws up her free hand to wave at me and pulls off. She's apparently concentrating on her driving more than she is on her phone conversation. Congratulations!

I'm amazed at the number of vehicles that are white-overwhelmingly so. Must be the visibility factor. White's good if you're traveling on black asphalt, but what if you're driving on an off-white concrete interstate? Maybe, with all the innovation in paint circles, someone will come up with a white paint that turns black when your vehicle comes in contact with concrete.

I think I've had enough, I believe I'll go to the house and take a nap. Wait, what's that? It's a young mother pushing a stroller in the street beside the curb. Kind of dangerous. Why isn't she pushing it on the sidewalk, where it's safer? Now I see why. The stroller looks to be too wide for the sidewalk. Holy cats, I believe she has triplets in that thing. Careful mom.

After retreating to the house and assessing my notes, I decided that group of drivers were not too bad. If I had to grade them I would give them an eight out of a possible ten. Except for the sweet young thing, they all seemed to slow down enough to avoid having an accident. After all, that's why the sign is there. The sign had done its job for this day.

Before leaving the stop sign subject I've got to tell you about an incident Annie and I witnessed last week. She had just had some blood work done and we were leaving the lab by the main entrance. We glanced left and saw this elderly gentleman, whom we assumed to be a disabled senior, riding a motorized scooter down the cement ramp into the parking lot area of the medical complex. Almost every parking space was filled, but there was no vehicular traffic at the moment. He turned right and approached a stop sign about 100 feet ahead. I didn't see a single vehicle moving. All was quiet. No movement. Perfect scenario for a quick glance left and then right and continue without even a slow down. Right? Not that guy. He stopped that scooter dead in its tracks, remained motionless for about ten seconds and continued his exit from the lot. Now, that's the kind of person the auto insurance companies like to have as customers.

*   *   *

Of all our traffic signs, we all know which one is most often broken-the speed limit. It results in more deaths than any other violation.

Most of our world seems to have become obsessed with speed. In some aspects of life speed is an attribute and is helpful in achieving our goals. This is especially so in the sport of professional racing-where speeds of 200 miles per hour are attained. Victories are achieved basically by three factors: driver ability, efficiency of pit crews and *speed*. Too much emphasis cannot be placed on the speed factor.

On our highways, however, disobedience of speed limit laws can result in tragedy. I saw some statistics recently dealing with causal of local area accidents. They showed that 50% of them were caused by breaking speed limits.

A large number of accidents involve just a single vehicle. More often than not it's driven by a young person who wraps the car around a tree while trying to negotiate a curve at too high a speed. If more of us obeyed speed limit signs, maybe we could reduce our vehicle traffic deaths below the 42,643 number for the year 2003.

I am amazed, or maybe dismayed, at the speed in which our products are delivered to retailers in order to reach consumers in a timely manner. It's good that this is being done efficiently, but sometimes I wonder if a method could be devised to accomplish this feat just as well in a safer manner.

At present, goods are delivered almost exclusively by humongous size trucks which we usually refer to as eighteen wheelers. And they can fly! They are so numerous on our interstates that it isn't unusual to have one in front of you, one back of you, and one beside you. You're outnumbered and engulfed in a feeling of helplessness.

To make a bad predicament worse, how about adding a concrete road divider about three feet away from the inside lane in which you are driving. Then, to make things even worse, a deluge from a thunderstorm is intent on drowning you. You're driving the speed limit-or five miles in excess-and driving conditions have definitely deteriorated. You would like to reduce your speed, but you can't. The big boy back of you is tailgating, wanting you to go faster, but that's impossible. The tires on the monster in front of you are throwing so much water on your windshield that you can barely see, even with your wipers gong full speed. The driver on your right isn't satisfied with driving 65 in this down pour that threatens to rival the great floods of history. He speeds up-faster is better. At some point in his passage, that tremendous vehicle pours so much water on you, you become totally blinded. I mean totally! For a second or two you cannot see a thing outside your little old private passenger car. You don't even have a chance to pray. Your hands are frozen to the steering wheel.

I have survived just such a situation-as many of you have-but it was scary. It was a time for slower, not speedier.

That problem is not going away. It's not going to improve with time. It will get worse. I read recently where one of our big carriers of cargo is planning to reduce its air cargo service and increase its motor carrier service. Wonderful! Great! We can't build highways fast enough now to accommodate the vehicles we already have.

We have to deliver our products, but is there a better way? We have all these great minds who have figured a way to send toys to other planets. Why can't some of that brain power be diverted to find a way to solve our huge, I mean really big, transportation problem? Mr. President talks about grandiose plans to construct a space station on the moon from which we can launch rockets to Mars. Hogwash! Why not spend that money on solving some of our domestic difficulties? I believe our average citizen would rather have it spent in that manner than on building a stairway to the stars. And do it with SPEED!

*   *   *

A sign we don't have on our highways, but maybe we should, is one that would read: "Don't Drive after Drinking".

Man's appetite for alcohol is sometimes insatiable-and it has apparently been for eons. I don't know if the liquid goes back as far as cockroaches do, but it goes back a long way.

In the Old Testament book of I Samuel, Hannah was praying silently. Her lips were moving but her voice was not heard. Eli thought she was drunk and he said to her "How long will you keep on getting drunk?"

Also, in the book of Isaiah these words are spoken of priests and prophets:

"And these also stagger from wine and reel from beer: priests and prophets stagger from beer and are befuddled with wine. They stagger when seeing visions, they stumble when rendering decisions."

This tells us that way back then people were partaking of drink in a way that provided intoxication.

When New York's Twin Towers collapsed September 11, 2001, due to the action of foreign terrorists, it was considered a debacle of major proportions-and it was. It resulted in the death of 3030 people. That was the first of its kind for this country. There will probably be more in time to come, but there hasn't been another within the fifty states since that date that I am aware of.

What has happened since that time, however, is that drunken drivers in this country have been on a killing spree. They have been killing our residents at the rate of almost two per hour. That means that by the fourth anniversary of the event, approximately 70,000 people had been killed in this country by drunken drivers. I wonder if road signs would have made a difference.

*   *   *

Sticker on the back window of a pickup parked in Wal-Mart lot: "I only ride my Harley on days that end with a "y"."

Church sign: Blessed is the nation that makes God its Lord.

Another church sign: In the beginning-God created.

If there were no signs in our country, can you imagine how total chaos would envelop us all?

CHAPTER TWO
LIFE IS — GLADNESS

I want to introduce you to a lady who, for ninety-five years, has lived a life of gladness on the bright side of life.

She was born in 1910 into a prominent farm family in Lenoir County, North Carolina. Life was good to her, living in a large farm home with grandparents who were able to supply all her needs.

At age 21 she flew the coop and married her childhood sweetheart. That was in 1931-in the middle of the Great Depression-and it was "root hog or die"-from that point in time. She worked at a number of jobs, one of which you won't believe.

She had her share of sickness and tragedy, but through it all she maintained a great outlook on life. And with the aid of a cane, she's still going pretty strong. Anytime I ask her how she feels, her answer is unequivocally, "I feel good".

I recently interviewed her and arranged a compilation of life highlights in a booklet I titled "A Journey". I presented copies of it to her and her three children at a party celebrating her 95th birthday which was held November 26, 2005.

I have chosen her as the person who personifies living a life of gladness.

My interview with her follows.

IT'S ALL ABOUT ATTIE

"O.k. folk, since Faye is sick and not available to play for us this morning, we'll just not sing."

"Wait a minute, Ray, I can play."

"Are you sure you feel well enough to do it, Attie?"

"Oh, yes, I feel good. I won't have any trouble."

"All right, get up there and tickle that ivory."

So began Sunday school for the Adult Fellowship Class of Northwest Christian Church on Sunday, March 13, 2005.

Faye Fields is our eighty-seven year old regular pianist who happened to be ill this particular day and Attie is her replacement on such occasions. I hated to call on Attie this particular day because she had not been well for three weeks and I thought she might not have felt up to the job of piano player so soon after recovery. I had underestimated her durability and viability. She's only ninety-four.

Not only is she capable of doing the piano thing, she is also an active seamstress-regularly making smalls larger and larges smaller. What dexterity for a ninety-four year old. And I wish I had her hearing ability. It would allow me to turn my TV volume to the downside. She could probably hear a pin drop in the Tabernacle.

And if you think she sits in her apartment all day viewing television, you've got another think coming. She is on the go six days per week, taking Wednesdays off to rest and rejuvenate for the remainder of the week's activities. She is still active in a sewing club and a monthly participant in *The Love Group* at Northwest Christian Church. She is responsible for setting up meeting locations and arranging programs. Tell her where a Gospel Group is performing and she will be there. Ask her out to dine and she'll ask, "What time?" I doubt there's a restaurant anywhere nearby that she hasn't patronized, nor a menu she hasn't tried. She also bakes a delicious lemon pound cake for the ill and shut-ins, and she is on hand for every church function.

"Attie, what is your favorite food?"

"Fish stew, but I can eat anything."

"How about your favorite eatery?"

"Probably the Kinstonian Buffet, but Virginia Perry takes me to Bo Jangles a lot for lunch-and I like it a lot. I usually eat out about four times a week. The rest of the time I cook my own stuff at home. Breakfast is simple-I just have packaged cereal and toast. For my other meals I like to cook soup, chicken pastry, collards and fish stew."

"How about telling me something about your life, Attie? I don't get to talk to a real active ninety-four year old every day. When and where were you born?"

"I was born December 20, 1910, just three for four miles east of Kinston on Neuse Road, on a farm that has a lot of history behind it."

She was not boasting. There is a lot of history behind the Jackson-Vause farm and I have read much of it, some of which I will share with you.

The original Jackson-Vause farm was the land bounded by the Neuse River, Southwest Creek, and old Dover Road (currently highway 70). John Jackson purchased it on April 9, 1770, five years before the Revolutionary War.

For the next few years, the area around Kinston and Lenoir County was a busy place, during which time Richard Caswell, Governor of North Carolina, made Kinston his state capitol. In this period, John Jackson and his wife, Cateron Arendall, were busy raising a family.

Between the years 1771 and 1784, three sons were added to their family household: John II, Jacob and Jesse.

The area in which they lived was raided twice in 1781 by British forces. Their objective was Caswell's Mill, which was producing musket balls and corn meal for the Continental Army. The Jackson farm, itself, escaped the British wrath.

The farm was passed down to John II around 1800. By that time the Jackson family had become influential members of the community and one of Jesse's sons became a charter member of Wake Forest College.

The farm came under ownership of John Jackson III about 1830, during good economic times for the family. Cotton was the big farm crop during that period and was very profitable. It brought a need for an increase in the number of slaves needed for planting and harvesting. There was a need for the Jackson children to work also. In 1840, John III was father to seven children and owned fourteen slaves.

A railroad link between Kinston and New Bern ran through the southern part of the farm in the 1850's. The future looked bright for John III when his daughter, Adaline, wed Robert Bond Vause in 1854.

When the Civil War broke out in 1861, it brought an abrupt halt to prosperity on the Jackson farm. When Union troops occupied New Bern in March 1862, Kinston's rail link to the coast was cut.

Federal troops raided the Kinston area in December of that same year. They had to pass through Kinston in order to reach their ultimate objective of Goldsboro, situated about twenty-five miles west of Kinston.

Local Confederates began constructing a line of defense fortifications along Southwest Creek, which extended along the eastern boundary of the Jackson farm and which are still visible. That fight has become known as the First Battle of Kinston.

Not only was the war disastrous to the family from a financial standpoint, it also brought a personal loss.

Robert Bond Vause had enlisted in a Confederate Heavy Artillery Unit and was killed February 18, 1865, near Wilmington, North Carolina.

During the Reconstruction Period following the Civil War, there were many changes to the Jackson place-and the huge profits that were once there became greatly diminished.

When John III died the farm was in debt. However, two of his grandchildren-Jesse Vause and William H. Jackson-paid off a property lien on May 21, 1877, in order to maintain control of the 564-acre farm. A third grandchild, John Irvin Vause, purchased 187 acres from the two boys for six hundred fifty dollars in January 1882.

John I. Vause married Attie Elmore in 1885 and they had four sons: Robert, Joel, Roland, and Carl. Robert Frederick Vause would father two daughters: Attie and Freddie. Attie was named for her grandmother and Freddie was named for her daddy.

John I had overcome a lot of adversity in his early life. His father had been killed in the war and his first wife had died in childbirth, after which the infant died some months later. His survival instincts served him well in later life. In addition to farming, he developed a house moving business to supplement his farm income. This would serve the Vause family well in the next generation.

The cotton industry declined in Lenoir County in the early 1900's and was replaced by tobacco as the leading cash crop. Some cotton was still planted, however, resulting in the family's construction of its own cotton gin.

The house moving business also boomed in the period between 1915 and 1921. That occurred when construction of hard paved surface roads necessitated the moving of many existing structures off the highway right-of-way.

John I suffered a heart attack in 1922, while moving a residence to make way for Kinston's first gasoline station, resulting in his death. He died at home.

The Vause farm was divided between John's three sons: Joel, Roland and Carl. Joel sold his share to Roland, as did Carl. The Vause family has now retired and the farm is leased to others.

"All right, Attie, now that we've covered your rather extensive family history, what say we get going on your personal life?"

"Well, I was born on the family farm in 1910, as I mentioned earlier. I missed being a Christmas baby by only five days. My parents, along with some other relatives, lived with Daddy's father at the time of my birth. My daddy's name was Robert Frederick Vause, but he died of a ruptured appendix at age 24, when I was only two years old-so I do not remember him at all. I was the first born to the family, but Mama was pregnant when Daddy died, so I soon had me a sister. Guess what her man was? How about Robert Freddie Vause? She was named after Daddy and I had been named Attie Elmore Vause after my granny.

After Daddy's death, my granddaddy, John I. Vause, told Mama he would take care of her, Freddie and me and we wouldn't need to worry about food, clothing or a bed to sleep on.

He was a good man and nobody could have been a better daddy to me than my granddaddy, who led a very busy and fruitful life. In addition to owning a large farm, he was also a house mover and even sold sewing machines as a young man. He used a horse and buggy and plied his wares over a pretty big area. I understand he met Granny while working one of his routes.

About a year after Daddy died, Mama started going out with a man named Ike Griffin, and they got married when I was about five years old.

Granddaddy didn't like Ike, so he was not invited to move into the house with the rest of the family. Ike was told that he and Mama would have to look for their own place, but Freddie and I could continue to live with him and Granny. We were glad to hear that, because we loved both of them dearly.

From that time on, I would sleep with Granddaddy and Freddie would sleep with Granny and that was a good arrangement. It allowed me to never have anything to do with my step-daddy.

* * *

After about a year or two after Mama married Ike, she came to our house one day with a mule and a cart. She told Freddie and me to get our clothes and get on the cart. She was going to take us home with her. What a sad day!

None of us had been told that this was going to happen. Neither Granny nor Granddaddy ever dreamed Mama would come back for us. The four of us were as happy as larks-not a worry in the world. I don't know what Granddaddy would have said or done if he had been home when Mama came to get us, but he was out working. I don't know if he could have persuaded Mama to change her mind, or not.

It was the custom back then for children to stay at home until they got married. We considered Granny and Granddaddy our parents, not Mama and Ike. We loved them dearly and had expected to stay right there in that big old house with people we loved.

Granny started crying while getting our clothes together for Mama. Freddie and I were just two little kids. What choice did we have but to go with Mama?

It took some time for Granny to get all our stuff together, with all the crying she was doing and we did not want her to hurry up.

When the last box was loaded on the cart, Freddie and I got on it too. That was when the two of us started crying-and we really cried. You would have thought somebody was whipping us with a lash, with all the wailing going on. The farther we got from the house, the louder we cried. We never let up. We were not crying in order to get Mama to turn around and take us back. We were crying because we were brokenhearted and terribly sad. Nothing could have been worse for Freddie and me at that moment than what was happening to us.

To this day, I don't really know why she did what she did. She knew we didn't like Ike and she should have known there could never be a peaceful household made up of the four of us. I don't know if Ike had any influence on Mama's action.

Then after riding about a mile on that tobacco cart, something unexpected happened. Mama said "Whoa" to the mule and the cart stopped! We were not even in view of Mama and Ike's place, what was going to happen? Was it possible she had changed her mind? Had the mule come up lame? Was the cart wheel about to come off? We stopped crying.

Then the most wonderful thing took place. We saw Mama turn the cart around and within a few seconds we were headed in the direction of Granddaddy's place. We were going home! Was it because she was tired of hearing our bawling? Could it have been her conscience getting to her, knowing she was doing something wrong that would make life miserable for her two little girls? We never knew the reason why. We didn't care.

When we got turned around, Mama said to us, 'I'm taking you back home and I'll never come to get you again!' I had never heard more joyous words. When we reached the yard, Mama started crying and Granny started up again. This time she was shedding tears of joy, no tears of sadness. We grabbed our bags off the cart and ran into the house. What a happy day!

* * *

It was good to get back in that house with all those rooms, plus an attic big enough for all of us kids to play in. It was a good place to play "house" with doll babies. We would also gather green moss from the tree trunks and wet places on the ground, take it to the attic and make play carpets out of it. There was an old sewing machine up there and I began tinkering with it before many years passed.

There was a huge fireplace in the sitting room and a smaller one in another room where we had a piano. We depended on the fireplaces for our heat and the men folk would put big oak logs in them that would burn all night. The heat from them, plus several blankets or quilts, made the house tolerable during the cold winter months. The fireplaces were also great for popping corn. With me sleeping with Granddaddy and Freddie with Granny, we got along just fine during extreme weather.

There were some things our grandparents insisted we do, and one of them was to attend church regularly at Southwest Christian Church. Both of them were devout in their religious beliefs, so I was brought up in Christian surroundings. There was no profanity or anything like that in our household-and we learned at a very young age to trust and believe in God. I have been told that Granny helped in a financial way to save Southwest Christian Church during the Great Depression.

They also wanted us to work in the fields during the summer months with the laborers, in order to experience what life really was on a farm. In addition to helping with tobacco harvesting, I also worked in the cornfields to gather fodder for animal feed during the winter months. That involved gathering cornstalks by hand and storing them in barns.

We were taught to handle a horse and buggy rig, too. In fact, Freddie and I were given one for our personal use around the farm and neighborhood. We used it to carry water to the laborers in the fields and to make short visits to friends and neighbors. There was something unusual about our rig though-the horse was blind."

"Attie, how did you manage it, if the horse was blind?"

"Well, that was not as big a problem as you might think. I controlled him with the reins. If I wanted to turn left, I pulled the left rein and said 'Haw'. When I wanted a right turn, I pulled the right rein and said, 'Gee'. When I needed to stop, I pulled both reins and hollered, 'Whoa'!

We were given custody of the rig when I was about eleven, I believe, and we had to learn how to grease the wheels and to do other little things to keep it in working order. I also had to put the horse's collar on. In order to do that, I had to pull the horse up beside a fence post. I then climbed the fence, stood on top of the post and slipped the collar on."

"Speaking of the Depression, Attie, did it affect your family adversely from a standard of living standpoint?"

"No, Ray, it didn't. We had good shelter and plenty of food. We grew corn and potatoes on the acreage, and we also had a big garden where we grew everything else we liked.

We made our butter and lard, milked our cows, and killed our chickens and hogs. Feeding ourselves during the Depression was no problem. We even created our own salt pork, which we ate and used for seasoning. We did it by putting a layer of fat pork in a barrel, then covering it with a layer of salt. We followed that procedure until it got near the top of the barrel. We then filled the barrel with water until it covered the top layer of the meat. Then we dropped an egg into the water. If the egg floated, it meant that the mixture of salt and meat was correct. If the egg didn't float, we would need to add more salt. When we got the mixture right, we would put a wood lid as a barrel top to float on the water so that the meat would stay under the water all the time. We would then cover the barrel top with white cloth to keep bugs out.

We bought such things as rice and flour by the barrels full in Kinston and hauled them to the farm by horse and buggy. We usually bought enough at one time to last us through a season.

Keeping ice on hand in the summertime was something of a problem. We would go to the icehouse in Kinston and buy a whole block of ice, wrap it as best we could and take it to the farm. We would then push it into a bin filled with sawdust, which was partitioned off at one end of the barn. Sawdust was good insulation.

* * *

Hog killing was a special day at our house, as it was for all farmers. Neighbors helped neighbors. We would kill as many as 25 or 30 hogs in one day and from them we would get enough country ham, sausage and other pork products to last us for a year. We also made our own lard by cooking hog fat and draining it. Thanks to our hog killings, we were able to have ham, eggs, rice and biscuits six days a week for breakfast. Sunday breakfast was special-that was when we substituted steak for the ham.

Our noon meal, which we called 'dinner', consisted of ham, rice, biscuits, sweet potatoes, butter beans, corn and cornbread. We had leftovers for supper."

"What about schooling, Attie, how much of that did you get?"

"Well, I attended Mill Branch School in grades one through six. It was only about two miles away from home, which allowed us to walk there. On rainy days Uncle Roland would let us take a mule and cart to get there and we picked up other children in the neighborhood who lived between our house and the school. It was just a small two-room frame building. The boys had the job of building a fire in the wood heater each morning before classes started. The teacher would excuse two or three of the boys from class long enough for them to go into the woods and pick up enough dry limbs to put in the stove to last until we were dismissed for the day. We tied the horse to a tree so he would stay while we were in school. We also carried a little hay and a few ears of corn to feed him while we ate our lunch.

After finishing sixth grade, I entered the seventh at Contentnea School where I stayed just one year. The school was located several miles north of where we lived and we rode the school bus-something new and enjoyable to me. That year, 1925, was the first year I studied music and piano.

For grade eight through eleven, which was all we had then, I attended Southwood School. It had just been built and it was very nice.

I became one of nineteen graduates of the High School Class of 1930. As far as I know, I am the only survivor of that class.

After Granddaddy died in 1922, Uncle Roland took care of Freddie and me. He was the one responsible for me taking piano lessons. He asked me to do it so I could play for services at Southwest Christian Church, which I did many times-both piano and organ.

Granny lived many years after Granddaddy died. She suffered from Diabetes and finally died of a stroke in 1950.

When I graduated from high school Uncle Roland offered to send me to college, if I wanted to go. I was more interested in getting married than I was in getting more schooling."

* * *

"Attie, when you were growing up out in the country as a youth, what was it like, compared to today?"

"It was nothing like today. We didn't have plumbing on the farm until after World War II. Until that time, our source of water was from a well, usually dug close to the house, if the well diggers determined sufficient water was available in that spot. We also had a hand pump installed on the back porch. It usually required priming to produce water.

Our toilet facilities consisted of two outhouses back of the main building-one for men and one for women. They were referred to as 'two-holers', meaning they could accommodate two people at the same time. Unheated, they were not places where you wanted to spend a lot of time reading Sears-Roebuck catalogues, even though we kept a small stack of them in each structure. They were forerunners of toilet tissue and were placed within easy reach of the holes. It was important to see that the supply of pages never ran out in the female latrine. As for the men, they could substitute corncobs for pages in emergencies. What a happy day it was when we could enter a room, do our thing, and simply hit a handle to clean the toilet bowl. And what a comfort it was to see a roll of toilet paper just inches away.

Another benefit we got by installing plumbing was the big improvement in our bathing procedure. For all those years we had kept a wash pan in our rooms to take 'cat baths' with, which was not a very good way to keep clean in the winter months. I remember Granddaddy, even in the coldest weather, going out on the back porch at the pump every day before dark to wash his feet.

During the summer, though, things were better. The men built a platform on the sunny side of the barn to support a big barrel of water. A pipe was inserted in one side of the barrel near the bottom and extended through the side of the barn into the inside of the barn. A big bucket was hung over the pipe in such a manner that allowed water to run out of the pipe into the bucket, which had holes in the bottom. It created a shower of sorts. The sun would warm the water sufficiently during the day to allow comfortable showers by days end.

You can imagine what a joy it was when we were able to turn a knob and fill a bathtub.

You might wonder what we did at night concerning toilet facilities. Now, that was another ball of wax. You can imagine some of the pitfalls you could run into by jumping up from a sound sleep running in the dark to find the latrine. To avoid that, in our rooms and usually under the bed, we had 'slop jars'. I feel like there must have been a more discreet word for those things, but I never heard of one. They were a type of bucket with a lid and were usually kept out of sight until needed during the night. The same instrument,

only smaller and made for children, did carry a more refined name-
a 'chamber'. Children used them day or night. We hoped that we
would need them only occasionally, but at times they became very
useful on a frequent basis, especially after taking a large dose of
castor oil before bedtime. It seemed like we took a lot of that stuff
back then. Not only did they give it to us for constipation, it was
used to 'clean us out' in almost any little sickness. I hated it worse
than anything! It made it a little easier to take, though, if you bit into
an orange as soon as you gulped the mess down."

"What about living in a house with no electric lights, Attie? How
did that work out?"

"Well, if you never had to do it, you probably think it would be
mighty inconvenient, but that was simply a way of life for many
years and we just made it do.

We had kerosene lamps in every room, which gave us sufficient
lights to do what we had to do. The lamp bases were filled with
kerosene and had a wick stuck in it. The other end was outside the
base and could be adjusted up or down as needed to give a brighter
flame and light. These are still used today in emergencies and do
quite well.

Still, it was mighty nice when we were able to just flip a switch
and at once be covered in brightness. I believe we got electric lights
about the same time we got plumbing. After getting both of them,
we felt kind of like we had moved into another world."

* * *

"Our family was noted for being the first ones in the neighborhood to do a number of things. The one I especially remember was the purchase of an automobile by Granddaddy. But I don't believe he drove it. Uncle Roland was the regular driver. It was a Model-T Ford but I don't remember what year it was.

When tobacco was introduced to our part of the state, farming changed completely. It was the crop that brought in the big money. But it sure took a lot of labor to grow, harvest and sell. Just about everybody in the family, except Granny, would get involved in it one way or another. Also, laborers-sometimes whole families-would be brought in to help harvest the golden leaf.

The job I liked most as a teenager was to drive the mule that pulled the tobacco truck between the rows of ripe tobacco. The 'croppers' would throw the leaves into the truck after stripping them from the stalk.

The truck was nothing but a simple four-wheel cart built about a foot off the ground and fitted with curtains made of tobacco sacks. The curtains went all around the cart and were about three feet high. They kept the leaves from falling off the cart.

I also got involved in 'looping' the leaves onto the tobacco sticks with tobacco twine. We then hung them in tobacco barns to be cured. After being cured four or five days, we had to take it out of the barn, separate the leaves into different grades and then tie them into bundles. The last act was to take them to a tobacco warehouse to be auctioned off to various tobacco companies.

The menfolk did the 'cropping' of the leaves because that was the hardest job of all-often performed in 90 - 100 degree weather. Working in tobacco was considered the hardest kind of labor on a farm in the early years-and I was glad when I left it."

"Speaking of labor, Attie, what kind of jobs did you hold down after you left the farm?"

"I had a lot of jobs after finishing high school. The first one was sales clerk at Rose's Five and Ten in Kinston. Rose's stayed opened until 6:00 on weekdays and 10:00 on Saturdays. But I didn't stay there very long. During that period, I stayed with my Aunt Lena Hill who lived in Kinston. She took in sewing for a living and she was the one who got me interested in sewing.

* * *

Ray, let me tell you about my wedding. When I reached the age of 21, Milton Wiggins-a boy I had known all my life-and I decided to get married. We didn't tell anyone ahead of time. When I packed my suitcase and left the family home, I mentioned to an aunt that I wouldn't be coming back. Milton and I grew up in the same area and we saw a lot of each other. I never seriously considered going with any other boy. When we grew older, we just assumed that we would get married. That time came when I was 21. There was no formal 'will you marry me, Attie?'

Granny really didn't want me to get married. It was not that she didn't like Milton-she just hated for me to move away from her. She allowed him to visit me on Wednesdays and Saturdays and sometimes on Sundays. Milton and I would be in the sitting room and she would be in the next room. At exactly 9 p.m., Granny would make a trip to the back porch to get a drink of water. That was a signal to Milton that it was time for him to leave-and he abided by the unspoken rule.

Aside from 'dating' at home, we would ride around and often wind up at 'Kelly's Mill', which at that time had a dance hall. The pond is now often referred to as Lakeside and is without a dance hall.

In those days a person had to pass a physical before a license to marry could be issued. Usually it took a day or two for this to be handled. Milton and I went to Dr. Hardy's office to have the physicals done. He told us to come back the next day and he would make the necessary marriage arrangements. The next day we met Chester Walsh, a local radio announcer and Justice of the Peace. He was the one who tied us up, after a brief delay, which was brought about by us having only two witnesses, when we needed three. Milton ran out on the street and grabbed a friend named Oscar Waller and brought him in to meet the requirement. The ceremony was performed on the date of September 19, 1931. We didn't know it at the time, but Chester forgot to fill out the marriage certificate to be recorded. This came to light years later when our daughter, Betty, applied for a job with Western Union and had to furnish them with proof of age. No birth certificate could be found. Then, when an attempt was made to verify her age through family records, nobody would find legal evidence of our marriage. That was when we discovered that Chester had never prepared the certificate. Finally, we got a local attorney, Marion Parrott, to get the whole mess straightened out. Years later, Marion saw me on the street one day and hollered out, 'Attie, are you still living in sin with that man?'

JOBS

The sewing experience I had gained at Aunt Lena's began to pay off. I learned enough to make my own dresses out of feed sacks and in later years I would make them for my children.

During World War II I worked for Marvin Vick at Sanitary Dry Cleaners. My job was sewing stripes and patches onto military uniforms that were picked up from Camp Lejune and brought to the Kinston plant for me to do the job.

Later in life I got a job as seamstress at Belk-Tyler's in Kinston. It was there that I worked under a nice lady who was an expert in her field. She graciously took me under her wing and taught me how to do better work in a shorter time. Her name was Ethel Carraway. It was then that I really began to enjoy my work as a seamstress. I worked at that job from about 1964-1968. I then had the opportunity to transfer to the store's piece goods department and work under Hazel Davis. Working under her for ten years was the most enjoyable work experience I had ever had. Belk-Tyler's policy at that time required employees to retire at age 65 and my time came in 1975.

In between jobs, which happened a lot, I had babies. Betty, my first born, came the year after we were married. Then came Myrtle, John, and Frances.

Myrtle died of cancer at age 62. Betty married Biggie Kilpatrick, who died seven years ago and she still lives in this area. John and his wife, Marie, live in Houma, Louisiana. Frances and her husband, James A. Taylor, live in Rose Hill, North Carolina. John and Marie make regular trips to visit me, even though it is a two-day trip each way. I see Frances frequently, and each summer our Love Group goes to her house to pick blueberries.

Over the years I had several other sewing jobs. One was at Pressley's Laundry and Dry Cleaners. Another was at Batt's Cleaners. But I didn't limit my jobs to sewing ones.

Milton's trade was bricklaying, which required us to move around a lot. At times, just before World War II broke out, he had a chance to do brickwork on a lot of houses being built in Jacksonville, North Carolina. The houses were to be occupied by military people to be stationed at Camp Lejune. We lived there for about 18 months. While Milton was laying brick during the day, I was home preparing meals for 18 laborers who were working with him. I saw no reason for me not to make money the same time Milton was. I cooked breakfast and dinner for the men, but no supper. For breakfast, I usually cooked grits, eggs, hot biscuits, bacon or sausage. I always had molasses and preserves. One man also requested black-eyed peas. For the noon meal, I cooked such things as black-eyed peas, collards, cabbage, turnip salad, Irish potatoes, fat back and pork chops.

The two of us also moved to Raleigh later in life and worked at a Methodist Home for children. We looked after 13 boys.

Later on we moved to Durham and managed a cattle and chicken farm for about five years. After that we moved to Sand Hill, close to our roots, a few miles east of Kinston.

I suppose the most unique job I ever had was being a 'chicken picker'. That was the name I gave it and it lasted about three months. It came about at a time when grocery stores started selling fresh cleaned chickens out of their meat coolers. I went to T. W. Daughety's Grocery on Fridays about noon and cleaned and bagged exactly 100 chickens.

There was a laundry and dry cleaning business next door to Daughety's that used steam. There was a pipe inserted through the wall that extended into Daughety's building, allowing the steam to escape and then turn to water. That water was hot enough for me to dip the chicken in, allowing me to pick the feathers. After the feather picking, I would gut the bird with a sharp knife and clean it out and wash it. I would then cut the feet off and put the finished product into a plastic bag to be put in the cooler and then sold. I would stuff the feet in a grocery bag and take them home. I would cook those things with rice and they became a delicacy. I was paid ten cents for each chicken, which meant I had made ten dollars for just a half days work. That was really big money for that day and time. My daughter Betty helped me at times."

* * *

Before the picking and cleaning of the chickens ritual could get underway, of course, an initial procedure had to be performed. The bird had to be executed.

How many of you have ever killed one, except by running over one with your car? I've killed a few in my lifetime, but I never enjoyed it. In those early years, if you wanted to have fried chicken for dinner there was a procedure to be followed. Somebody had to go to a grocery store and purchase a live chicken. There were a number of them in a coop and you had your choice of picking out the one that looked the best to you. It was somewhat akin to picking out lobster at the present time. When the chicken was decided upon, the store clerk would cut a hole in the bottom of a brown bag, stick the bird's neck through it and hand the bag to you. It was then up to you to determine how to exterminate that domestic fowl. No asphyxiation. There were two ways to get the job done: chop its head off or wring its neck. To me, neither was pleasant, and sometimes it wasn't easy. Chickens were sometimes like humans-they attempted to delay death as long as possible.

And that brings to memory an instance years ago when Polish jokes were prevalent around the country.

It seems that three men: one French, one German, and one Polish, formed a gang of three. They rampaged across Europe committing robberies, killing people and raping women. They were finally caught in France, found guilty in French courts and sentenced to death by guillotine. On the day of execution all three were brought out and lined up in front of the killing machine. The Frenchman elected to be the first to go. He walked up to the base and was approached by the executioner, who asked, "Do you wish to lie down facing the ground, or do you want to look at the blade?" "I want to look up. I've always wanted to see things when they were coming at me." After strapping him down, the trigger was pulled and that heavy blade, positioned between two grooved uprights, came hurtling down. The Frenchman's eyes as big and white as golf balls were glued upon it. Suddenly came a loud 'pop'. The eyes of all spectators were focused on the Frenchman's head. It was still in place. It hadn't rolled away like it should have. All eyes then shifted to a spot just above the head. There, as if suspended in space, was the blade, just three inches short of its intended victim. There was a malfunction. It had happened previously. The executioner reached down, untied the ropes and pulled the trembling man up. "This is your lucky day-the law stipulates that when this happens the prisoner goes free. Get out of here!" A maintenance man examined the apparatus, fiddled with it a while and declared it to be in good working order. They brought the German up. "What do you want-face up or face down?" "I want to be face down. I don't want the last thing I see in this world to be a big, wide and slanted blade headed full-speed in the direction of my throat." The same ritual of tying down and releasing the blade on the Frenchman was followed with the German. There was the same result-a loud 'pop' and the blade stopped three inches short of its target. Another lucky criminal was released. Prison authorities, intent on executing somebody, ushered the Polish prisoner to the designated spot. Again, the executioner asked, "Do you want to be tied face up or face down?" "Neither one-I'm not getting under that thing until you people get it fixed!"

* * *

I don't believe I've ever liked to kill anything of much size, and that includes chickens. I like to eat them, especially fried, but I've always preferred for someone else to kill and prepare them. There have been times, however, when I couldn't avoid the task. And I can recall one such occasion.

I grabbed that chicken's neck and began whirling her around in about the same fashion drivers used years ago in turning a crank to start a Model-T Ford. After making enough revolutions to break the necks of a dozen chickens, I threw it on the ground and congratulated myself on a job well done. When I started to turn to go into the house to tell Mama that the job was done, I noticed movement from that hen. In a few seconds it had slowly scrambled up and attempted to walk. I quickly grabbed it by the legs, picked up a hatchet with the other hand, placed the bird's head on a wood block and whacked it! The job was completed. Messy, but done.

Fortunately for Attie, she was no amateur. She knew exactly how to grab that neck and in one whirl, break it, bringing death quickly.

She couldn't' afford to mess around when she had one hundred bodies of poultry to dress.

* * *

"My final regular job lasted twelve years and was most enjoyable and different. I was a daytime nanny for Warren, Jr. and Stewart Perry's children: Warren and Andrew. A great friendship developed between the Perry family and myself. The boys still call me 'Granny'."

"I believe I've just about run the gamut, 'Granny', except for covering your health. I know you've had some illnesses. How about telling me about them?"

* * *

"Yes, I've had sickness, of course. My first occurred while I was working at Sanitary Cleaners. I began putting on a lot of weight, almost as if I had become pregnant and my stomach looked like I was. I must have reached 160 or 170 pounds, but I knew I was not pregnant. It turned out to be a tumor discovered by Dr. Jean Smith. She performed a hysterectomy and took out the tumor that weighed eight pounds. I was in the hospital for six or seven days and I didn't work for about a year. The surgery was successful and I made a full recovery.

While working at the Methodist Home in Durham, I had a hernia to rupture. Surgery was performed and that was taken care of.

In about 1976 I had gallstone surgery performed by Dr. Frank Sabistan and that problem was taken care of with the removal of my gall bladder.

In 1997 I had a pacemaker installed and some other work done that resulted in a hospital stay of forty-three days. I've had the pacemaker battery replaced just once, a few months ago. When it was first installed, I was also put on oxygen and was told I would probably have to stay on it permanently. However, I was able to get off of it in about nine or ten months. That problem had been brought on when my heart began leaking into my lungs. I had to spend six or seven days in intensive care.

In 2004 I was hospitalized for fourteen days with a staff infection and just a few weeks ago I was hospitalized with a urinary infection. I've recovered now, and am just about back in my usual routine."

"Attie, do you ever worry about death?"

"Heavens no. I'm not worried about that or anything else. I've been so fortunate in life that I've got no concerns about the rest of it. I have really been blessed.

I moved into this Kinston Towers apartment twenty-five years ago and have been here longer than any other tenant. At times I think about how nice it would have been to have Milton up here with me, but it just was not meant to be.

Diabetes can be such a horrible disease. It finally cost him both legs and put him in a nursing home. It was there that another terrible disease, cancer, finally took his life at age eighty on November 9,

1984. He had not been able to overcome cancer as he had done to his first impediment in life-being club-footed. His right foot was turned in to some extent and nothing medically was ever done to get it corrected. In his teens he began turning that foot in his every day activities and through pure determination, he gradually turned that foot around over a period of years. He was able to hold down full time jobs until his final illnesses.

I have everything in this little castle that I need, heat in the winter and air-conditioning in the summer. I have facilities to cook, eat, and sleep. I even have sitting space for my friends to visit.

Even though I've lost Milton and Myrtle, I still have my other children around me. With all these things going for me, plus faith in God, why should I worry? I now have complete contentment. What else could anyone ask for?"

*   *   *

I recall an old song of many years ago that contained these words...

'Get your coat and get your hat,

Leave your worries on the doorstep.

Life could be so sweet, on the

Sunny side of the street.'"

"Certainly, **Attie Elmore Vause Wiggins**

has lived her life on the 'sunny side of the street'

and is the personification of the bright side of life.

God Bless You Attie,
&
Happy Ninety Fifth Birthday
November 26, 2005

CHAPTER THREE
LIFE IS —A TEST

Most of us are bombarded with tests of some sort from the time we enter kindergarten, at least that's what I'm told. When I entered school there was no such thing as kindergarten, so far as I know. I'm glad there wasn't. I never was totally enamored with school anyway and I was glad to get a diploma for finishing eleven grades. At age five I believe I would have preferred going barefoot and playing kid games than I would have sitting in a classroom.

After failing second grade, I passed enough tests to graduate with the 1942 class of Grainger High School. My first test after my diploma that was presented to me occurred at Fort Bragg, N.C., when I was inducted into the United States Army. I apparently scored enough points to convince the military establishment I was not a total imbecile-and that I could be taught how to fire a gun. I passed the first test of my adulthood.

My first test after military service came about when I applied for a job with Retail Credit Company, which entailed making inspections for insurance companies to determine if applicants for insurance coverage should be accepted or rejected. Actually, that test wasn't one to cause a great deal of anxiety. It was one that asked a few questions about my educational background and health. It didn't take long to furnish them with my educational history.

I was also asked if I could type. When I answered "no", I was asked if I could teach myself to type within a short time. My answer was "yes". They apparently were desperate for bodies which could walk, talk, and determine which block to check when recommending an applicant be rejected or accepted by the insurance company. When I resigned that position a few years later I had become one of the world's fastest hunt and peck typists.

Inasmuch as I had no desire to further my education beyond high school, I was never involved in taking the SAT tests. It's a good thing!

Then, there are other types of tests. Remember that expression: "He was put to the test?" It usually referred to somebody who had accomplished some unusual feat. Lance Armstrong would probably fall in that category for his many victories as a professional biker. Sir Hillary would also be in that group as a mountain climber.

Sometime back I read a book that told the true story about how seven men and a young female were put to a test of their own choosing, one that would cost them their very lives, should they fail.

"The Long Walk" is a wonderful book that illustrates how much the human body can endure and still survive.

I have never known the will to live to be as graphically depicted as it was by Slavomir Rawicz in this book.

He was a young Polish Army officer who was arrested by the Russians in 1939 and charged with committing espionage against the Soviet Union. It was a trumped up charge that resulted in imprisonment.

At his trial, in which no real evidence was presented against him, he was found guilty and sentenced to twenty-five years forced labor. Within a few days, he, along with hordes of other prisoners, was herded into train cattle cars which were built to haul eight horses or cows each. Every car was jammed with 60 men. It was so crowded there was no room to sit down. Everyone had to stand the entire time. There were no toilet facilities.

After months of traveling by train and foot they reached their destination. It was prison work camp 303 in Siberia-the world's coldest country-located 350 miles south of the Artic Circle. They were all physically spent when they arrived there.

Rawicz began thinking about escape as soon as he regained his strength. He solicited six other prisoners and they managed to escape during the second week in April during a heavy snowstorm which prevented guards from seeing them.

In each man's pack was a loaf of bread, a little flour, about five pounds of barley, salt, a small portion of tobacco and newspaper. On top of each pack was a spare pair of moccasins. Those were the provisions with which they hoped to survive the harsh conditions ahead of them-if they were to survive.

They crossed the Lena River, their first objective, about eleven days into their journey. It was there on that body of water, frozen solid, that they experimented with a trick of survival Rawicz had heard about in Poland. One of the men found a solid piece of timber in nearby woods. They walked about 20 yards onto the ice and began using the log like a battering ram, and finally broke through the ice. At the moment of breakthrough, the water gushed up like a geyser. It must have resembled Old Faithful at Yellowstone. Water shot up and landed all around their feet and-yes-four fish came out with the water, fresh seafood to please the pallet.

A few signs of spring were appearing in mid May and things were looking up. Despite their attempt to avoid human beings, it was impossible to do so forever.

Some weeks after the fish affair they came face to face with another Homosapien, a female, no less. A 17 year old named Kristina. She was Polish and had been sent to a work camp in another part of Siberia, from which she had just escaped. The men assured her she would not be molested by them-and they invited her to travel with them. She happily accepted their offer and would remain with them until her death months later.

*   *   *

A milestone was reached when they entered the country of Mongolia. What a welcome to be out of Siberia.

After crossing the Mongolian border they were deluged with rain that lasted two days without ceasing. When it did stop they entered the Kentei Mountains, which took about eight days to negotiate.

It took about eight weeks after entering Mongolia for them to reach the country's Gobi Desert. At the time they entered it none realized the hell they would have to endure in order to survive the huge expanse. At that moment they had no water and little food. They were in an area where some of the greatest fossil finds in history had been made, including the first discovery of dinosaur eggs, but this fact was of no interest to them at the moment.

What they were really concerned about was the size of the area and its geography. And its climate. Its area is more than 800,000 square miles and its climate consists of great extremes and can vary from -40°C to 45°C.

It is inhabited by such animals as gazelles, polecats, snow leopards, brown bears, and wolves. It grows several shrubs adapted to drought conditions and low grasses such as needle grass and bridle grass. The Gobi is not a typical desert as most people envision one.

There are some areas with abundant sand, which can breed sand-storms, but a great deal of the area is covered by bare rock. Some sections of the desert include mountains and some areas are blessed with ponds and streams. The strictly desert portion of the Gobi is crossed by several trade routes that have been used for thousands of years.

Most of Gobi gets less than eight inches of rain annually but parts of it receive less than two inches.

Needless to say, the Gobi desert would be a mammoth test for the group to pass through in order to reach their destination.

Shortly after entering the Gobi, their supply of dried fish became exhausted-and there would be no food or water for the next six days. Seven males and one other plodded over boring landscape, barely able to put one foot before the other, and stumbling at times. Miraculously, on the 6th day an oasis came into view. "It's a miracle", whispered Kristina, "God has saved us."

After a day and night at the oasis, they decided to move on. Six days later they buried Kristina. Months of trials and tribulations which had been endured with seven wonderful men had ended. She had simply collapsed due to complete exhaustion on a desert floor thousands of miles away from home. Her escape from prison had ended in death.

Four days after Kristina's death, the first male died. Sigmund Makowski, age 37, had stumbled a number of times that day and had to be helped along by the others. After being laid down for a short rest, he failed to get up. Life had expired. The group, which at one time consisted of eight, now numbered six. Who would be the next to succumb to the rigors of the sojourn?

Thirteen days away from the oasis-and no water, if none could be found within the next twenty-four hours, Rawicz figured it would be death for all of them.

The water they found was not really water, but mud that contained a bit of moisture. The men stuck their faces in the mud and sucked. For a few minutes they acted as if insane. They chewed the mud and spat out the gritty residue. One of the men, the American, took his sack off his shoulder and put a corner of it in the mud. When the sack became soaked he sucked at the wet corner. The others followed his example and it resulted in just enough water to give them hope.

By following that slit of mud, they finally came to a place where water collected in tiny pools, true life-saving water, a little bit at the time.

The problem of food had to be solved if they were to remain alive. The only live thing they had seen in days was snakes. They decided to see if snakes could become the lifesaving food they so desperately needed.

They fashioned a forked stick which they would jam down below the snake's head. Then another of the group would cut its head off. They picked up small pieces of scrap wood with which to cook the snake after skinning it. A diet of snakes saw them through the Gobi.

*　　*　　*

When they reached the mountains of Tibet, their water shortage ceased. They didn't usually have to go more than a day without the liquid.

The date now was about October 1941. They had about fifteen hundred miles of difficult Tibetan country to traverse in order to reach the Himalayas.

They yielded to the urge to stop and take advantage of the generosity and friendliness of the Tibetan villagers. One such person gave them good advice about passing through the mountains looming before them. He instructed them to never get too tired to build a fire. If they should go to sleep with no protection against the forces of nature, they would not wake up. The night they spent with this gracious person was the first time they had slept under the roof of a house since their escape.

It must have been about the first of December when tragedy struck again. Finding a shallow cave as shelter from a rainstorm, the six men built a fire and settled down for a fitful nights sleep. At daybreak, and time to arise, Zaro stumbled over to where Zacharias was sleeping. "Come on, Zacharius, get up!" There was no movement. Another call for him to wake up, but no response. Rawicz went over, examined the body and declared that Zacharius was dead. He was only about twenty-nine, but he had given up the struggle for life.

There was no place to dig a grave in the rocky soil, so they placed his body in a cleft between two rocks and threw pebbles into it to fill the space above the body.

Late January 1942, they came upon a great river completely iced over. Winter had overtaken the men and temperatures at night were below zero. Snowfalls were heavy, as was the sleet. Wind was strong.

In February, they entered their last village, which consisted of eight or nine houses. They were all two story, the only ones they had seen with more than one story since their prison exit. They were ushered into one of the homes and greeted with the same cordiality they had received from other Tibetans. They were given hot tea and fed with mutton. The event was one to be remembered by both hosts and guests alike for many years. Tibetans filled each man's sack with food to take with them, and even cooked a young sheep. While it was cooking, feet were being doctored. When the five left they were loaded down with food, including a complete side of cooked sheep. They were waved farewell by the villagers with the words, "God be with you", ringing in their ears.

*　　*　　*

At the end of March they felt sure they were near India. But they still had the highest peak to conquer. One more great effort was needed to get them to ultimate freedom.

At the top of the last peak they had to spend the night on a flat ledge where snow was piled up. They dug a hole several feet deep in the snow for protection through the night. There was no fire and they could not afford to let themselves go to sleep. It was the longest night either of them had ever spent. Next day's light was surely welcome.

They came in contact with two huge creatures not long after beginning the new day's trek, and that forced them to revise their original route down a deep slope. It was an incident that would bring final disaster to the shrunken party.

They were at the end of a slope during their descent when a loud cry was heard-and Paluchowicz was missing. He had fallen into a bottomless chasm and nothing could be done to recover the body. The tough old sergeant had departed the world so close to success. He had possibly lost his life due to a careless mistake.

They had been without food for about eight days when they completed their descent. At once they saw a flock of sheep with men and dogs in charge. The final four must have looked like skeletons, but at that moment their fear of recapture was gone. They were in the safe haven of India.

Twelve months earlier seven men had a choice to make. They could remain in a Siberian prison camp-and possibly die there-

or they could face the toughest test of their lives in attempting an escape. They wanted a chance at a better life, so they made the decision to escape. That decision meant walking four thousand miles under extremely difficult conditions in order to gain freedom.

Marchinkovas, Makowski, and Paluchowicz failed the test. Rawicz, Smith, Kolemenos, and Zaro passed it and lived.

All seven men were possessors of the highest degree of a will to live.

CHAPTER FOUR
LIFE IS—A MIRACLE

There are times when I believe miracles do occur, but I probably don't have as much faith in them as some people. I do, however, believe in bible miracles. Maybe my faith in "everyday miracles" is tarnished somewhat because I've witnessed too many strikeouts. I can recall some of the occasions when I was in special prayer groups to petition God to save lives of young people. They had been terminally ill with cancer or some other dread disease-and our entreaties did not produce the results we hoped for.

There are, nevertheless, innumerable documented cases of miracles occurring regularly. One such is "Overboard", by Bennie Shipp-reprinted with permission from "Guideposts". Copyright © 1964 by Guidepost, Carmel, New York. 10512. All rights reserved. It follows:

I remember how badly our kids wanted to go fishing with us that November morning. The two boys tried to talk us into letting them skip school, and even the little girl was for it. But of course we said no.

My wife and I always went fishing Mondays. I'd shut down my filling station and we'd haul our outboard to Lake Chickamauga. This particular Monday was gray and raw. But that meant good fishing, and we'd have the lake to ourselves.

Sure enough, when we reached the beach there wasn't a car or boat in sight. We pushed the boat into the water, I got the motor going, and we were off, without so much as a frown over the fact that Vivian couldn't swim a stroke and wasn't wearing a life jacket. Funny how you figure some things just won't happen to you.

Vivian had brought a coat for me to put on, but I couldn't take time before starting. Seems like I couldn't wait to get to a spot I knew where I could just smell those big black bass waiting for us. Out on the water, though, it was a lot colder.

We were moving along pretty well, maybe 18 miles per hour, and the wind was fresh.

"You'll catch cold!" Vivian hollered over the noise the outboard was making.

Well, I reached for the coat, and I guess I gave the tiller a twist, because that boat gave a terrific lurch. I was holding on so I didn't fall. But Vivian was thrown from the seat into the water.

I choked the motor down, never taking my eyes off the spot where she went under. Then I dived in. I swam straight down, looking for her through the brown water. I saw her, got my arm around her and started kicking for the surface. We broke water just when I thought my lungs would burst.

Vivian was wonderful. She didn't fight me or grab me the way some people would, she just lay back on my arm and I saw she was praying. I looked around for the boat. I couldn't hold her up much longer with our heavy clothes soaked with water.

I couldn't see the boat. I turned around the other way, figuring the dive had mixed me up. I made a complete circle in the water. There was no boat. Then I saw it. It was 200 yards from us and moving away fast. In my hurry to get in the water I hadn't shut off the motor all the way: the boat was gone and so were we.

I saw Vivian had seen it now, too, but she just whispered, "God's going to take care of us, Bennie."

Well, I knew I couldn't take care of us much longer, that was sure. The shore looked a million miles away. There wasn't a sign of anyone else on the beach, and even if someone came right now, by the time they could put a boat in the water and get out to us, it was going to be too late.

It was the weight of our clothes plus the ice-cold water that made it so bad. I knew we had to get Vivian's coat off. I got my arms under her shoulders and she wiggled and tugged at the heavy, clinging thing, and we both swallowed a lot of water. But at last she broke free of it.

But getting my boots off was a different thing. I had on the high laced shoes I wore at the filling station and they got heavy as iron and dragged me down. I tried to get one hand down to undo the lace, but Vivian and I both got ducked. She had had all the water she could take.

She wasn't scared, though, not even now. "God's going to help us," she said, over and over.

Well, Vivian seemed so sure I began to figure how maybe God could do it. Perhaps He could send a sea plane and set it down on the water beside us. But the only things in that gray winter sky were a few birds.

I was too tired to hold my head out of the water all the time. I sank down below the surface where I didn't have to kick so hard in those iron boots, holding Vivian up above me. Every little while I climbed up and got a swallow of air. Each time it seemed as if I wouldn't make it.

And then I knew I was dying because I could see my whole past life. And it wasn't much to look at. Not until two years ago, anyway. I saw the years I'd spent stock car racing, the money I'd wasted, the heavy drinking, the close calls racing a car after a few drinks.

And I saw Vivian, the way she'd been all those years. She'd never given up on me; she'd just kept on praying for me. No matter how late or how drunk I'd come home, she'd have dinner hot and waiting. And no cross words either, just:

"God loves you, Bennie. He's waiting for you."

Then one night, two years ago, I'd come home at 2:00 a.m. when the bars closed, and there was Vivian just sitting and waiting as she always was. And suddenly I knew she was right about God because no one could be as good as Vivian on his own. I got down on my knees then and there and gave my life to Him....

I swam up to the air and breathed for a while, remembering these things and the wonderful family life we'd had ever since. I hauled one of my boots up as far as I could and clawed at the water. I didn't think I'd make it to the top again. My arms ached with holding Vivian above me.

Well, it was God's life now and it was all right for Him to take it anytime. I just didn't like to think about the kids, coming home from school, and us not there. I was too tired, too tired to keep struggling. I thought I could sleep-except that Vivian was pulling at me, tugging my arm. She was shouting:

"The boat! The boat!"

Now I saw something moving on the lake. I couldn't make out what it was at first, but it looked as if it was coming nearer.

"It's the boat!" Vivian said.

It couldn't be. But it was, our own empty boat, somehow turned around and headed straight for us. I knew it couldn't happen. But I was seeing it. And even then I didn't dare hope I could grab it. I didn't have any swim left. That boat would have to come to the very square foot of water where we were for it to do us any good. If it was even three feet away it was going to pass us by.

I watched it come, moving straight as if a sure hand were on the tiller. And suddenly I knew-sure as I'd ever known anything-that boat was coming right to us.

I just lifted up my hand and my fingers closed over the side of it. It was the last strength I had. I couldn't do any more for a long while than just hold on. Vivian had more strength than I had by then. She climbed aboard and shut the motor down. And for a long time I just hung on. Then, when I was rested a bit, I climbed in too.

Well, we sat there, water streaming off us, and we just shouted for joy. Then we sang for joy. Then we prayed for joy and just magnified God in every way we knew. Vivian saw I was rubbing my arms and she said:

"Bennie, it wasn't God alone. You held me up till He could come."

But I shook my head, "You've held me up too, Viv. I was thinking in the water how you prayed for me all those years when I couldn't. Well, I was just swimming for you, when you couldn't."

And I guess that's about all we can do for each other, just hold one another up, until God provides the help we need.

*   *   *

The Old Testament is filled with miracles performed by God which resulted in creation of a free Israel. And God even bestowed the ability to perform miracles to his prophets-even the miracle of life renewal. Two such instances are shown below.

People of the city of Jericho complained to the prophet Elisha: "Look, our Lord, this town is well situated, as you can see, but the water is bad and the land is unproductive."

"Bring me a bowl", Elisha said, "and put salt in it." So they brought it to him. Then he went out to the spring and threw the salt into it, saying, "This is what the Lord says: 'I have healed this water. Never again will it cause death or make the land unproductive.'" And the water has remained

wholesome to this day, according to the word Elisha had
spoken.

2 Kings 2:19-22

*   *   *

When Elisha reached the house, there was the boy lying dead
on his couch. He went in, shut the door on the two of them
and prayed to the Lord. Then he got on the bed and lay upon
the boy, mouth to mouth, eyes to eyes, hands to hands. As he
stretched himself out upon him, the boy's body grew warm.
Elisha turned away and walked back and forth in the room
and then got on the bed and stretched out upon him once
more. The boy sneezed seven times and opened his eyes.
Elisha summoned Gehazi and said, "Call the Shunammite,"
and he did. When she came, he said, "Take your son." She
came in, fell at his feet and bowed to the ground. Then she
took her son and went out.

2 Kings 4:32-37

In writing about prayer and miracles, I cannot leave the subject
without telling about a rather bizarre incident involving our Cindy,

which was included in an enlarged version in "They Didn't Bring Ice on Sunday".

She earned her special education degree at East Carolina University and her Masters at the University of North Carolina at Chapel Hill. She then obtained a teaching position in the Wake County, N.C. school system.

Except for a bout, or two, with intestinal influenza as an adult, she had always been in good health until late 1985. She became extremely ill one day while teaching, resulting in her aide driving her to Rex Hospital in Raleigh. They performed x-rays, scans and other procedures and came up with a diagnosis of uretal pelvic junction obstruction. They found she also had cystitis and inflammation of the bladder. All this resulted in a need to drain infection that had built up in the kidneys. They also found she was the owner of four ureters, whereas most people have only two. Doctors then discovered that a vein had been lying across one of the urethras long enough to shut off the urethra tube. This caused a backup of urine in the kidney, forming an abscess. She was advised not to return to work, instead she was to come home with us and begin taking antibiotics to build herself up physically for surgery in January 1986.

Those few weeks at home became an important time in her life. Not only had she been successful in gaining needed strength, she also became engaged to a young man named Edward Demianiuk- from Chicago. He was a student at the University of Illinois who had spent the past summer working at the veterinary school at N.C.

State University-he had been housed in the same apartment complex as Cindy in the City of Cary.

In January, as scheduled, she entered Rex to have the necessary surgery performed. The operation consisted of going in and removing the damaged portion of the urethra, putting a stent in it and sewing it back together.

Surgery was successful and they inserted two catheters for drainage and sent her to a room for recovery. I was there when they returned her and I noticed the two tubes were draining as they should. But it wasn't long before I noticed one had stopped. I commented to the nurse it surely had drained in a hurry, causing her to check it and say, "It hasn't finished draining-something is wrong."

This was a problem we didn't especially need. My experience with hospitals up to this incident had been limited to an appendectomy stay by my wife before our marriage in 1947, plus an appendectomy to our son, Mike, before he was a teenager. I really had not been around a lot of sick people-but I could tell things were not going as they should have been for Cindy. Instead of her outer appearance improving, she was looking worse and her tone of voice appeared to be getting weaker.

Doctors and nurses began coming in to check her and all seemed at a loss as to what to do to correct the situation. One doctor performed a reverse flush and water went through the other end, indicating there was no obstruction inside the tube. When he ejected the needle, however, nothing happened-still no outward flow. Her sick sounding voice was getting worse and at about midnight the nurse asked me if she should call the doctor at his home. Even though I hated to do so-knowing the doctor had worked all day and surely needed his rest-I said, "Yes, please."

The doctor instructed them to have a MRI performed as soon as possible. It was about 1:00 a.m. when they rolled her up to the machine and slid her in. To while the time away, I walked around the hospital halls, including a stop in the hospital's chapel.

When they had completed the MRI, I accompanied them back to Cindy's room. There was little sleep that night. The next morning I was told the MRI had revealed nothing that could cause the problem. I was informed later in the morning that doctors were hesitant to perform more surgery due to her weakened condition. Nothing good was happening. Everything seemed to be in suspense-nobody knowing a solution to the problem.

*   *   *

In looking back on your life, do you ever think about the little incidental events that occurred over your lifespan? I mean the ones that were not important at the time but had a tremendous impact on your life later?

I think about myself-I would not have met and married Annie Phillips had I not been riding around with Robert Simmons one night. He decided to stop by a boarding house to see if any of the girls wanted to go for a ride. Annie was one of them

I also think about our fifty-year-old son, Mike, who might still be a bachelor had he shopped ten minutes earlier or ten minutes later in that supermarket in Asheville about four years ago. That was where he saw for the first time Helen Carlton and her two children, Jane and Ryan.

The destiny of many of us is determined by chance meetings which we had never anticipated occurring.

*   *   *

On that January day in 1986 Cindy was a participant in a happenstance event that would become extremely beneficial to her well being.

One of her friends, who had lost a child sometime back due to spina bifida was subbing for her at school. She came for a visit and during the course of conversation she said to Cindy, "Cindy, life's not fair." Truer words were probably never spoken. After a short while she opened her purse and pulled out a big handful of cards. She handed them to her saying, "Here are some get well cards the children made today", and waved goodbye.

Remember now, Cindy was a Special Ed teacher, which meant children in her class were directly diverse from those in "gifted' classes. I understand they can come up with some things that will break your heart-or cause you to erupt in laughter. Thank the Lord for the latter.

I wish I could remember just some of the remarks they wrote on those cards and some of the figures, that in looking at them and reading them, I thought they were the funniest things I had ever seen. They really brought forth the belly laughs I had stored in me. Someone once said laughter is contagious, and it must be. When I finished a card I would pass it on to Cindy, who would read it and join in the laughter. After a few cards we were both laughing so hard we were shaking and this continued until we had gone through every card.

When I started putting the cards back in the box, I happened to glance down at the defective catheter. It was draining! Hallelujah! Cindy's voice changed almost immediately from a sick sound to one of recovery.

Isn't life strange? It's possible for us to be transformed from a joyous moment to depths of despair in the wink of an eye. That moment, in that hospital room, the reverse occurred. Gloom and doom were thrown out the window, making room for sunshine and happiness to enter through the door.

When the last day of recovery arrived and the doctor came in to discharge Cindy, I asked him to tell me exactly what had happened. What had caused the problem and what had cured it?

His explanation was this: "The only possible explanation is that somehow during surgery I must have cut a tiny piece of flesh that was sucked to the opening of the urethra when the drainage began flowing. It's similar to a leaf stopping up a small drain. When Cindy started laughing so much that her body shook, it must have caused that flesh to move off the hole, allowing drainage to resume." "But," I asked, "why didn't the reversed flush do the trick?" His answer, "The water did push the obstruction up enough to open the hole, but when the reverse flow stopped it must have settled right back over that hole." His last words to Cindy were, "Cindy, when you get back to school, thank your kids for those cards. They very possibly saved your life." Was that occurrence simply a coincidence, or did a higher power have a hand in it? Yes, prayers had been lifted up for Cindy.

I recently brought up the subject of miracles to a friend, whereby, he recounted three phenomenal experiences he has been through in his life.

Many of you will regard at least two of these incidents as being absurd, fictitious, poppycock, ridiculous or just plain falsehood. If I did not know this man as I do, I might feel the same way.

LESLIE

Les and I have been close friends for many years. Our relationship had its birth about fifty years ago at Gordon Street Christian Church-and continues today at Northwest Christian. Our kids grew up close to the same time. He and I played in the same golf four-some for years. We also rotated teaching Sunday school for quite some time.

He is a devout Christian who makes prayer an important ingredient of his daily life. He prays over every major decision he makes. I believe every one of the incidents he related to me.

Incident #1-"Lissa was born in 1951 and at age 2 was stricken at home with an extremely high fever. We were unsuccessful in reducing it, so we called a next door neighbor, Mrs. Parnell, who was a nurse. She suggested putting her in cold water in the bathtub, but that was also to no avail. Finally, our family doctor, Z.V. Moseley, was contacted-and he brought in Dr. B.C. West for consultation. Shortly, the two arrived at a diagnosis of spinal meningitis.

Our child was hospitalized and her room quarantined. Dr. West worked with Lissa into the night, but was unsuccessful in his treatment. He finally gave up, saying to the nurses there was nothing else he could do-and asked them to let him know the time of death-if it should occur during the night.

At the time this was going on, a group of parishioners were meeting at Gordon Street Church for special prayers on our behalf.

She didn't die that night. Next day a blood transfusion was decided on, but the doctors needed a special strain of blood which was rare. It was a type that would coagulate faster than the regular type. Certain people around town were blessed with this blood and made a practice of volunteering it when needed. Doctors Moseley and West were discussing in the lobby and just a few feet away a man was waiting for his wife, a nurse, to get off duty. He heard the doctors' conversation and approached them. 'You guys need some of that blood? I've got a body full.' The transfusion was performed and Lissa began her recovery.

My wife had a brother to die previously of the same illness." Everything had miraculously fallen into place.

Incident #2-"It was Christmas night at about 9 p.m. in the middle 1970's. We had been at one of our relatives houses for a Christmas meal and exchanging of gifts. There were about a dozen relatives there, plus the five of us. We had enjoyed ourselves, as we always did, when visiting Cove City relatives.

I was driving our 1970 Oldsmobile "98", west on highway 70. The year was about 1975. My wife and I were in the front seat. All the children were in back. I seldom exceed the speed limit, so I must have been driving about 55 mph. The children were always getting on me for being a slow poke. When we drove places in tandem we were always last arriving. At a spot about halfway between Cove City and Dover-approximately where Wells Lumber Company was- we met a row of four or five cars driving east on #70. It was a two lane road then. Just before we met, one of the cars pulled out of the line to pass the cars in front of him. I thought surely he saw me and would pull back inline, but he didn't. I attempted to avoid him by heading for the right shoulder, but there wasn't enough time. A near head-on was inevitable-but just before impact a strange thing happened. Everything seemed to change to a slow-motion mode-just like in the movies. Every move I made to avoid the crash or to protect myself moments before the crash was in slow motion. The impact was in slow motion.

His left front hit my left front. My car was totaled. There were no injuries in either car. The young man driving the other car admitted fault and apologized. He was returning from a Christmas party in Goldsboro."

Incident #3-"In the 1980's Cathy was teaching and living in Swansboro-only about 50 miles away-we made frequent visits there. In one of those visits we stayed a little longer than usual before returning home. I was driving a 1975 240-D Mercedes with Hazel beside me. The year was about 1983. We were driving on hwy 58 at my usual speed of 55. It was about 10 p.m. I remember being near a crossroad when, suddenly, I came upon several vehicles-no lights-in the middle of the highway. One was a wrecker that appeared to be hooking up to a disabled vehicle. I realized there was no room to go around the scene and there was not enough room to squeeze through the pileup. A perfect situation for disaster-but I found myself beyond the accident scene, driving at my normal speed of 55 on hwy 58. How did I get there? I don't know. Rationale tells me we should have been part of the pileup scene back of us-but we were not. I can't attribute either blessed event to life-saving prayer on my part. I didn't have time to pray. I didn't have time to pray in either instance.

I do know I have a guardian angel. It's a male and I even know his name, but I can't divulge it."

––––––––––––––

Over the years many books have been published dealing with unexplainable events, many of which occurred in and around World War II. I recall reading one many years ago that contained an incident I still recall above all others. Some of the pertinent details seem to have glued themselves to my thick skull.

It involved an occurrence during the Japanese-Chinese conflict in the late 1930's. Japan had invaded that huge country and was enjoying great military success and was capturing great chunks of Chinese soil. They were destroying everything in the army's path-devouring China's food crops, pillaging, killing civilians and raping women. In one of the sectors being carnaged by the Japanese, a children's hospital stood. Word reached the nurses in attendance that the enemy was headed in their direction. They were terrified, not only for their lives, but also for lives of the children. The institution had absolutely no protection from any source. There were no Chinese soldiers available for defense.

In due time the enemy, consisting of foot soldiers and armored vehicles, advanced close enough for the hospital staff to hear the rumble and clanking of the armored equipment. Soon they were sighted-hordes of them. Then suddenly something wonderful and unexpected happened. The vehicles stopped and engines were cut off. Foot soldiers ceased their motion-the entire army came to a standstill. What appeared to be a group of leaders emerged at the head of the column and seemed to be conversing. In a short time motors could be heard starting and hospital employees' hearts sank. Their worst fears were about to become reality. But wait, instead of continuing their march straight ahead toward the hospital, that horde of humanity made a column left. It advanced at a quick pace until it was completely out of sight. The hospital was never touched. What was the explanation for the Japanese action?

*   *   *

Years after World War II ended, there became times when military people on all sides came together under friendly circumstances and discussed their wartime actions in specific battles. It became a time for former enemies to become friends.

It was on such an occasion that one of the nurses, who was in the children's hospital that fateful day, came face to face with one of the Japanese soldiers who had been in the column that failed to attack the facility.

Nurse: "I was one of the nurses in the hospital that day. Tell me-why did your army suddenly stop and turn away without attacking us?"

Soldier:"When we got within sight of your building, we suddenly saw a huge army of soldiers protecting it on every side. It appeared much larger than our forces and we were afraid to attack."

Prayer

Therefore let everyone who is Godly pray to you while you may be found. Psalm 32:6

The vast majority of people in this world believe in God. In doing so, they then believe in an entreaty we refer to as prayer. Belief in God and prayer go hand in hand. You might say they are synonymous.

If you've never prayed, you might ask how to enter the procedure and what the importance of it is. What do you say to God and how long should you take to utter a prayer?

There are many different ways in which people pray. The New Testament tells us that during the time of Jesus the Pharisees, an ancient Jewish sect, had a habit of finding a public place and praying for long periods of time. This seemed to impress others with their religiosity. Jesus suggested going to a quiet place to communicate with God.

There are long prayers and there are short ones-and I suspect God recognizes them all-as long as they are rendered in earnest.

I saw an old movie sometime recently starring Clint Eastwood, James Garner, Tommy Lee Jones and Donald Southerland. They portrayed astronauts of years past who were suddenly asked to go back in space to repair a Russian station that had been armed with nuclear warheads. It was now plagued with mechanical problems-making it a danger to Earth unless it could be repaired quickly. It was determined those four guys of the geriatric generation were the only group who could do the job soon enough to save earth's inhabitants.

After a short refresher training period, they entered the space-craft and were strapped in their seats awaiting liftoff. One of the group asked, "Hey guys, you think a short prayer might be in order?" Garner spoke up, "Yes-Lord, don't let us foul this thing up." Short and to the point.

Prayers are personal to each individual and vary in content. Some people have a tendency to save their more fervent ones for "big ticket" items in which they pray for physical healing. Some pray for help in particularly hazardous situations-letting nightly prayers and meal blessings suffice at other times.

Many others pray for small things, such as praying for good weather when an outing is in their plans. Some pray for help in selling a house, or to heal a minor cut. Some make prayer a necessary part of their daily lives, asking for guidance in every decision they make.

Our daughter, Cindy and her family, fall in this group. When the kids come down with colds, they treat them and immediately pray over it. If they plan an outing, she prays for good weather.

She and the three kids were down from Wisconsin a couple of years ago and wanted to see a Kinston Indians baseball game. It would also give them a chance to observe the July 4th fireworks display.

Since they were down to Atlantic Beach for a few days prior to the 4th, it was necessary for me to procure game tickets on July 3rd. I visited the ticket office and asked for five tickets, however, I was told they didn't have five seats together. I had to accept two seats in the very top row, two in row F and one in row E.

Michael and Lauren ran up to the top row and settled down. Cindy, Katie and I stopped at row E, where I had a ticket for the end seat, but it was occupied by another gentleman. I checked my ticket, looked at him and said, "Sir, I believe you are occupying my seat." "Yes, I am, but my wife's ticket is for the seat next to this one and I would really like to sit next to her. I have two tickets on row F right beside the two seats you already have. If you will let me keep this seat, I will give you my two tickets and all of you can sit together on row F." Done deal. That gave us four seats in a row-and there was an empty seat beside Katie's, making a total of five, we waved to Lauren and Michael to come on down and sit with us, enabling the entire family to enjoy the game and fireworks together. What a nice turn of events. After the game I mentioned to Cindy how lucky we had been to get the seating arrangement we wound up with. Her comment, "Oh, daddy, I prayed about that." "What do you mean you prayed about it?" "I prayed that somebody would offer us seats so we could all sit together."

A great number of prayers fall in the intercessory category-praying for good things to happen to someone else. The bulk of these prayers probably occur in churches, where prayer lists are printed in weekly bulletins for congregations to see and act on. Many individuals whose names are not on those lists are also recipients of such prayers. As a religious nation whose motto is "In God We Trust", we do not hesitate to pray for anything and everything. Sometimes our prayers are answered and sometimes they are not, notwithstanding the fact many people say all prayers are answered, one way or another.

I have been interested in events of the American Civil War in recent years. Focusing on the religious aspect, it appears that leaders on both sides of the conflict were confident God was on their side and would reward them with victory.

In a movie some years back pertaining to that hostility, both Stonewall Jackson and Robert E. Lee were portrayed as men of God. As Confederate generals, they both relied on prayer before battles.

Jackson suffered a serious wound in the Battle of Chancellorsville which resulted in his death a short time afterward. When he realized the severity of his injury, he asked his wife to pray for him to live-but he also reminded her to include the phrase, "Thy will be done."

A few hours before Jackson's death an aide went to General Lee and advised him of the imminent death of his good friend and top commander. General Lee's response was, "No, he can't die. God will not take him from me just when I need him most."

I have wondered at times if the Battle of Gettysburg, that was fought not many weeks after Jackson's death, would have had a different result had he not died.

Some of us hesitate to pray for good things to happen to us-such as wealth, good health and blessings untold. Some regard it as being selfish, and we know how God hates selfishness. There is, however, precedent for this type entreaty.

In 1st Chronicles, chapter four, there is a long list of clans of Judah that covers several pages. At the end of verse eight the writer interrupts the genealogy chain to insert the following paragraph: "Jabez was more honorable than his brothers-his mother had named him Jabez saying, "I gave birth to him in pain." Jabez cried out to the God of Israel, "Oh that you would bless me and enlarge my territory! Let your hand be with me, and keep me from harm so that I will be free from pain." And God granted his request.

To me, it seems strange this little short historical note would be inserted to interrupt a genealogical list. But I understand this was not too unusual in the near east writings of that time. I can find nothing else in the Bible regarding this person, Jabez. The writing must certainly have great value, however, in order to be included as a portion of the Old Testament scriptures-and it sheds more light on the subject of prayer.

I consider prayer to be a spiritual communication between mankind and God. It's a great benefit humanity derived from the crucifixion of Christ, when the temple's curtains were ripped apart. To Christians, that act opened a line of communication between individuals and God that had previously been open to a select few.

CHAPTER FIVE
LIFE IS — THE DOCTOR'S STORY

∽०∾

‍‍‍

Over the years I have watched with interest an occasional TV religious program that featured divine healings. There were cripples being healed on stage, legs being lengthened, arthritis being cured and various other miraculous acts occurring before my very eyes.

I always found myself wondering how many, if any, were genuine and how many were pure fraud. I recently saw some so-called healings exposed by one of the television networks, so my suspicions must have had some merit-to say the least.

Real miracles do occur, of course, but there is one type illness I've never heard of being cured-in any way-until recently. That's mental illness. This incident involved prayer and is genuine. Isn't it strange that it would occur right here in "my own backyard?"

The recipient of such a blessing is one whom I became acquainted with in third grade of public school. We then remained in essentially the same classes through high school and were fellow graduates of the Grainger High class of 1942.

We both returned to Kinston after military service-and from there both of us pursued different careers, but both of us remained here in Kinston. He became a physician and would later become pediatrician to my children.

He has recently completed a publication entitled "How the Cross Can Make You Free from the Law of Sin, Sickness and Death." He has allowed me to include a few excerpts in my manuscript. They follow-and what you read is factual.

Biography

Richard Thornton Hood, Jr., was born in Kinston, North Carolina, attended the local public schools, Davidson College, graduated from Duke University and Bowman Gray School of Medicine of Wake Forrest University. After internship and residency training at the Medical College of Virginia and the New York Medical College he returned to his hometown and practiced pediatrics and pediatric allergy for 15 years. He then discontinued general pediatrics and practiced allergy and immunology in children and adults for 17 years before retiring. He served in the Navy during World War II and the Air Force during the Korean War.

THE ODYSSEY INTO HELL.

A. Panic!

He was a small white boy, perhaps 2 ½ years old, very pale, sweaty and breathing rapidly. He had gotten into a large bottle of flavored Baby Aspirin tablets and eaten them like candy several hours before he was brought to the hospital. By the time we got him, he was already hemorrhaging from his rectum and gums and was in marked acidosis. His blood pressure was low and his veins collapsed. So I began to do a "cut-down", a procedure I had done numerous times when it was necessary to get intravenous fluids (I.V.) into a small child quickly. He needed immediate blood, sodium lactate, and glucose which I had readied. I located the Saphenous vein just in front of the tibial malleolus on the inside of his ankle and I made an incision over this vein, with the help of a fellow pediatric resident physician. I was freeing it up so as to be able to insert a plastic I.V. catheter into it. I noted that Dr. Lee Sutton, the Chief of the Department of Pediatrics at the Medical College of Virginia (MCV) and two or three of the local Richmond pediatricians unexpectedly had come onto the scene and were intently watching. I was preparing to nick the vein and thread the I.V. tube into it when I first noticed my heart pounding and sweat beginning to run on my face. I looked again at the older pediatricians who seemed to be studying me and felt an unfamiliar emotion at such a time-it was fear. I didn't know why-what I was afraid of-but it was rapidly building in me, racing away with me, consuming me. I thought, "God, what is happening to me? I've got to get out of here!" I gave the I.V. catheter to my physician helper and held the vein so that he could easily slip it into its lumen and start the fluid. Thus, I quickly managed to switch myself from being in charge of the procedure to becoming the assistant. He swiftly concluded the matter, tying the catheter into the vein as I started the fluids running. My panic had increased and all I thought of was getting out of there and escaping to …oh, anywhere!

I ripped off my rubber gloves and left the room leaving my "assistant" completely in charge. No one seemed to notice as I swiftly left the room, escaped down the inside flight of steps connecting the 9th floor pediatric section of the hospital with the ground floor. I could not use the busy elevator for by now the panic was almost complete and the sight of any human was so frightening as to be intolerable. I knew no one would be on the stairs and I'd be free to go all the way to the ground floor and to my room in the residents' quarters without being seen. Irrational fear flooded my brain as I fled down, stopping only when I collapsed from panic on the 5th floor landing. I had already diagnosed myself: anxiety state with panic attack. I knew how I'd treat myself, if I could just get the medicine. I pulled myself up and gently pushed the door open and, seeing no one, slipped out. Then, way down at the very far end of the ward a little student nurse stepped out of a room into the corridor. Panic again struck me like a bolt of electricity and I jumped into a closet and hid behind the door. After a moment, holding the door in my trembling hand, as sweat poured down my arms and chest, I peeped out. No one there. I was familiar with the 5th floor having rotated through it when I was "on Medicine" as an intern months earlier. I knew where the drugs were kept. I slipped out and quickly got a supply of Seconal (secobarbital) capsules. I wanted to get it into my bloodstream quickly so I chewed up the bitter 50mg. capsule, swallowed it and continued my flight down the stairs, gulping air all the way to my room. Collapsing on the bed, I tried to fight the fear that gripped every inch of my body, but the panic grew intolerable; I thought I was dying! But just then I noted just "a little piece of peace," and then another and another until it grew. Within five minutes I was transformed into my old capable, confident self again. Oh, thank God!

Such was the first forty minutes of an odyssey that was to be twenty-one years. This was late March 1951.

B. The Joyless Journey.

I had graduated from medical school three years before, served a one year rotating internship at the Medical College of Virginia Hospital in Richmond and was now finishing my residency training in pediatrics when this thing struck. I found the next day that the fear, that I had hoped I had chased away with Seconal, was very much present and had taken up residence inside me. The panic was never again quite as intense as it was that first day, and any time it started building I took just enough Seconal to stave it off. What I was left with between doses was a constant, unrelenting, grinding anxiety which made no sense for there was nothing I knew of to fear.

I reported to Craig Air Force Base Hospital near Selma, Alabama where I was made Chief of Pediatrics, taking my wife, Lou, and twenty-one month old son, Rick, with me. To prevent the anxiety from getting too severe, I had to take some Seconal almost daily. It was an extremely uncomfortable two years, but at the end I was offered the rank of major if I would stay in the Air Force. However, I wanted to go somewhere and find a cure and to spend another year in training. Dr. Sutton had welcomed me to come back to MCV for another year, but I was in doubt as to whether I could handle the more intense stress and responsibility which I'd have to endure in the teaching hospital. I went to Richmond to talk to Dr. Foster, my psychiatrist there, about whether he felt I might comfortably return to the hospital staff. After prolonged discussions, I found that just talking about the coming responsibilities made me anxious, so we knew I wasn't ready for that level of stress.

He recommended that I be admitted to the McGuire Veterans Hospital in Richmond for treatment first. I moved my wife, Louise, and son, Rick, now almost four, back to her mother's home near Reidsville, North Carolina, while I was admitted to the VA Hospital in Richmond. There I was placed on Insulin Subshock Therapy daily. Each morning an injection of insulin would force my blood sugar level down to just above the shock level, and I'd go to sleep, and upon awakening I'd be given a large container of super sweetened juice which would bring my blood sugar back up to a normal level. After this I'd be taken to hydrotherapy where I'd stand up naked against a wall while an attendant managed something that looked like a fire hose. He'd place the stream of water on me from my chest down to my ankles at great force while adjusting the temperature up and down but never burning me or make it unbearably cold. The force of the stream was always great. By the time he was finished, my skin looked almost as red as a lobster. My skin had been super stimulated to say the least. Finally, after about three weeks, I was discharged, but there was no real improvement.

I finally decided that I would go somewhere there was a large concentration of teaching hospitals. There I could join in with other pediatricians in clinics and seminars; and take various courses where I could function well but without the fear-producing responsibility of critical patient care. Yet I'd be increasing my knowledge for the time when I hoped I could go into my own practice without the crutch of a drug. This place had to be New York City where, on Manhattan Island alone, there were several medical schools and many teaching hospitals. There I wouldn't have to do a contracted residency in order to take part in the medical education but would be welcomed to limited participation in some of their activities.

First, I took a course in Pediatric Cancer at the Sloan Kettering Institute, later I took a course on laryngoscopy at the Flagg Institute at Cornell University Medical School. I developed a regular route of hospitals where I attended meetings, helping occasionally with patients and got to know the senior physicians. After a few months, having read Dr. Norman Vincent Peales' book "The Power of Positive Thinking" and knowing where his Marble Collegiate Church was located, I decided to go see him and ask if he could help me.

Upon entering the church office I was interviewed by several ladies who then referred me to their own Church psychiatrist, Dr. Smiley Blanton. I was seen at the church psychiatry clinic a number of times and then it was decided that I needed psychoanalysis. He suggested that I see a psychiatrist-analyst that the Church recommended who was from Czechoslovakia and who had studied under one of Sigmund Freud's first students. I went to see Dr. John Braun and then began almost daily sessions for the next two years. I never did get to talk with Dr. Peale, but was able to function without Seconal.

* * *

At about this time, after two years of psychoanalysis, my psychiatrist called my wife, Lou, in to see him, however this was unknown to me. He told her that, as she knew, I had panic disorder and also "psychotic depression" and in addition, he told her I had incurable schizophrenia. He recommended that she have me committed to one of two "excellent psychiatric institutions," both in Virginia where he assured her I'd receive "loving care for the rest of his life." He was willing to help by signing the commitment papers. She didn't believe him, and bless her heart, she never told me of this until many years later. My hearing this prognosis might well have shattered my faith and hope in Medicine and brought depression crashing down on me. Dr. Braun knew my innermost thoughts whereas I had hidden them from Dr. Ratner.

I fooled myself enough to believe that now I might successfully open an office in Kinston for the practice of pediatrics and pediatric allergy. We moved back home. After three weeks of practice I went into a combined depression/anxiety state and flew back to New York to try to get help from Dr. Braun. I was hospitalized in a private psychiatric hospital. I remember very little about that week which makes me think, since I improved, that I must have received electroshock therapy.

Returning to my Kinston practice I immediately began seeing Dr. Bernard Bressler, Associate Professor of Psychiatry at Duke Hospital, who treated me for the next sixteen years. He started by giving me antidepressant drugs. Depression had become the most prominent characteristic of my condition as time passed, though anxiety remained important. Over a period of years we went through all of the then known antidepressant drugs. As I took each one it seemed to help a little initially, but all ultimately became useless.

This was an exceptionally trying period for me because antidepressants generally gave me little or no relief. My distress was so great as to push me into trying other things on my own initiative. The Seconal had not helped my depression as it did my anxiety so I began to use alcohol increasingly at night. Having determined that I'd never drink during the daylight hours made it only more likely that I'd stay up later and later at night drinking. Finally it became so bad that I couldn't get up in the morning to go to the office until later and later each day. It came to the point that I'd arrive at my office near noon and find maybe thirty patients waiting to be seen. Amazingly, my staff and patients apparently never suspected a thing. But Lou knew the whole story and became increasingly distressed as my family life and marriage deteriorated. At one point, Dr. Bressler, unknown to me, suggested that Lou bring my local physician, Dr. Tom Parrott, into more active participation in my case so that she would have a second physician available to sign psychiatric commitment papers (as required by law) should they feel I must be "put away." Lou begged me to stop drinking, but my depression and anxiety were so great that I wasn't about to give up the one thing that seemed to make life anything other than utterly and totally miserable. We argued and finally I blew up and left home moving to the Hotel Kinston to live for a period. She then left home, taking our youngest, Ken, who was too young for school, to her sister's home in Roxboro, NC and Rick to another sister's home in Ruffin, NC where he was enrolled in school. After approximately six weeks I called and talked her into bringing the children and coming back home with me.

Somehow I had built up a large practice in a short time, but the depression kept me feeling utterly exhausted. For example, I expended no effort unless it was absolutely necessary. For many years, I was too debilitated to take a shower, so every three weeks or so I'd fill the tub with warm water and shake in some Tide detergent then lie motionless in it for a long time. Feeling too tired to scrub I'd rub my hands over part of my body, then using my toes I'd release the stopper and let the water run out. (It's amazing how much dirt Tide gets off that way!)

After a morning in the office I would have worked up a new allergy patient then come home to eat. After lunch, I'd take the patient's chart to bed with me and dictate my findings in a letter to the patient's referring physician. After a nap I'd return reluctantly to my office where I'd smile and try to give the impression that all was well. Apparently I was able to get by with it for we never had any indication that anyone knew what I was experiencing.

When all the available antidepressant drugs had failed, shock treatment (electroconvulsive therapy) was instituted. Over the years, Dr. Bressler had to admit me to the psychiatric unit at Duke Hospital on six to eight occasions, once for five weeks. Over a period of several years as an out-patient, I received thirty-two or thirty-three shock treatments for deep depression. This allowed me to discontinue excessive drinking.

*   *   *

After each shock treatment I slept for a while and upon awakening was extremely confused and groggy, had a severe headache and experienced temporary loss of memory. All lasting most of that day after which the deep depression was relieved enough so that I was able to go back to work again the next morning.

One day when I again realized that a deep depression was coming upon me, I was quite surprised to realize for the first time that I had suddenly grown quite afraid of having another shock treatment. I had no idea why I had this dread. It did not make sense to me. However, I knew I had to have a treatment because the depression was growing deeper rapidly. Prior to this I had always disliked it, but I knew it was just an unpleasant thing I had to go through, but it would be worth it to get relief. But now, I forced myself to go through with this shock treatment despite all the fear with which I was seized. It was horrible having such fear yet knowing that I had to get the treatment in order to get relief. Thereafter, I went into each treatment feeling like something dreadful was going to happen to me but not knowing what it was. This same dark foreboding happened to me each time I needed a treatment. Many months later, rather suddenly, in a sort of dream, I realized why I had such fear. In my "dream" I relived one of my treatments. During a shock treatment two things are done: first you are put to sleep with an intravenous barbiturate and when fairly deeply asleep, the effect of a second drug becomes manifest. The second drug is Anectine (succinylcholine chloride) which the psychiatrists like to call "a muscle relaxer" though it totally paralyzes every voluntary muscle in the body including the diaphragm with which you breathe. This is done so that when the electric current is shot through your brain and you would ordinarily have a violent convulsion when all your voluntary muscles go into maximum contraction, yet you are protected by Anectine from harm. Anectine paralyzes all the muscles so that the violent convulsion is impossible and it saves you from chewing your tongue or breaking your bones. If there is adequate barbiturate dosing, premature awakening during the treatment is never a problem. But since one has to have fairly deep anesthesia to keep from waking when the brain is greatly stimulated by the lack of oxygen from non-breathing, waking can on very rare occasions occur. Usually, nurse anesthetists give patients positive pressure air by face mask for the approximately five minutes that Anectine paralysis persists. But I had had so many shock treatments, using the barbiturate drug, that my body had built up a tolerance or resistance to the sleep-giving drug so that the anesthesia was too light for me. So what I experienced, but had forgotten, was that after being put to sleep and being totally paralyzed by the Anectine, I had suddenly waked up unexpectedly when my breathing stopped. I tried to tell the doctor, and then tried to kick and jerk my hands and arms and legs. Then I realized I could not speak, move or breathe. Totally helpless and not being able to breathe I was suffocating, and I panicked believing that I was going to die. About this time, I must have gotten the actual electric shock treatment because that's all I remembered. Unfortunately, I had not been able to remember this incident upon awakening due to the memory-destroying effect of the electric surge through my brain. Then when it came time for me to have another shock treatment for depression all I knew was that I was having a horrible dread of the treatment and I didn't know why. When the revelation suddenly came to me I called my psychiatrist and told him that during my treatments I had been waking up in this horror. I told him I felt certain that the resident psychiatrist, in charge of the treatment and the anesthetists on the shock team, did not know that I had been going through this experience, but it must have happened several times. I pleaded with him to raise the dose of the barbiturate, so that I'd never again have to be awakened when breathing was suddenly cut off, and I'd not again experience impending death. He complied. Initially, I feared he might not raise the dose high enough. But fortunately, I never had to endure this terror again.

However, several years later, after I was totally healed of the depression, I began having frequent nightmares in which I dreamed someone was choking me to death, and I would wake up fighting violently for my life. This was terribly frightening. I hated to go to sleep at night for fear of the horrifyingly real experience with impending death. I prayed to God repeatedly and the dreams finally ceased.

After a number of years it became obvious to me that the shock treatments were beginning to lose their effectiveness both as to their increasing frequency of need and the lessening of the degree of relief being obtained. My psychiatrist, as a last resort, suggested a new psychosurgical technique being pioneered by Dr. Thomas Ballentine, then a neurosurgeon at Boston General Hospital. There was nothing else he had to offer me. He obtained published reports on all medical knowledge of the operation of anterior cingulotomy, which was said not to impair one physically or intellectually, and suggested that I study it and make up my own mind. After long and painful study I finally agreed to turn my brain over to the surgeons. My faith in Medicine was great for I "just knew" that Medicine would help me some day. I flew to Boston accompanied by Lou and my dad where they shaved my head, and under anesthesia bored two holes in my skull, inserted two electrodes deep into my brain at a predetermined spot and cut on the electricity destroying the two small targeted areas of my brain. After surgery I noted great memory loss, some of which was never returned, tiny loss of sense of balance and some loss of position sense. As part of my post surgical memory loss I found I could no longer do math beyond the fourth grade level. But I ran across Lou's fifth grade arithmetic book and beginning from that point I started to learn math successfully with the help of books of higher grade levels as I progressed. I was finally able to do all the math calculations needed to prepare vaccines and calculate all other medical procedures needed. I didn't bother to go back to relearn trigonometry and calculus for I didn't need that, thank goodness! But as far as relief from clinical depression, there was absolutely no improvement!

C. Faith in Medicine.

When I first entered medical school, I recall that the only oral or injectable antibiotic drugs available were sulfa and penicillin. But by the time I graduated, we were using streptomycin, Aureomycin, schlor-amphenicol and a host of other new drugs. We were healing typhoid fever, tuberculosis, plague, spinal meningitis, Rocky Mountain Spotted Fever, all kinds of tropical diseases and a host of others were falling as modern medical knowledge of antibiotics, immunology, biochemistry and technology expanded and, with it, the death rates plummeted. New vaccines were being developed and many more diseases were preventable now. The treatment of several mental diseases began to improve as new drugs were discovered. All the frontiers of medicine were being breached and I saw disease going down to utter defeat as the men of medicine powered on victory on top of victory. I thought it the Golden Age of Medical Progress. Unconsciously, I developed the certain knowledge (faith) that medicine would inevitably conquer all disease. So dramatic was the progress that I became certain that ultimate victory was only a matter of time, perhaps only in a very few years. This was a heady time for this young physician-scientist just by being a part of this revolutionary triumphant profession. This faith affected my outlook toward my ghastly depression. During my medical training when I was working on psychiatric duty I rarely saw anyone in a depression as deep as mine. Yet I never doubted that a cure was soon coming for me.

When medicine repeatedly failed to heal me I was simply temporarily disappointed knowing that the victory was on the horizon as I started to take a new treatment. Never once in my twenty-one years of illness did the idea of suicide ever enter my mind that I can recall. All the while others with depression less severe than mine, (but without my absolute faith) were thinking of and frequently committing suicide all over the nation. Now, there is no doubt in my mind that I would have shot myself through the brain had it not been for the power of my faith. Listen folks, faith works, even my misplaced faith.

I had gone to the church in New York for help and they indicated that a "Christian" psychiatrist could do a better job than they could. Now, what was I going to do? I had given myself over to psychiatric treatment of all types available for almost twenty-one years, and physicians had tried and given up, having made it clear that the surgery was the last final best hope they had for me. My psychiatrist, however, agreed to continue to provide shock treatments if I wanted them. All I had to do was call and he'd schedule me for one, and have one of his psychiatric residents handle it. And over the next few months, I continued to need an occasional shock treatment.

My dad heard about Vernon Hall, a beautiful old twenty-five room mansion on thirteen lovely acres located on a hill overlooking the city of Kinston, which was then being used as a Christian mission. Dad understood that healing was believed to be important at the Mission so he recommended it to me. My faith in medicine had been shattered and hopelessness was taking on a whole new and dangerous meaning for me. I thought, "Hell, I've already flown up to Pittsburgh twice in order to have Katherine Kuhlman (the late evangelist famous for successful healings) to pray for me but it didn't help either time."

After I looked into the Mission and its leader, I reasoned, "Why should I go up and ask some uneducated sixth-grade dropout named Tommy Lewis who wasn't even ordained, to heal me?" He was in charge of the Mission, but I had known him earlier. He had been a bicycle repairman for a local sporting goods store and had worked on my children's bikes. Back then, he didn't even have a car or a bike of his own, but rode from his home in a "bad" section of town, to his job on one of the bikes he was repairing. My intellect cried, "Why in the devil should I waste my time going to this jerk?" After all, my therapists and preachers had all been highly educated and were well-qualified. They had come from "proper" backgrounds and from "good" families. Well, you know how a drowning man acts; he reaches for anything no matter how small and foolish it seems to be. So I reached forth for healing through Tommy Lewis for I had no other options left anywhere in the world. I had reached the bottom!

Tommy held six teaching meetings at "the Mission" a week on a regular basis and did a good bit of private spiritual counseling also. About three months after my failed surgery, I began to attend the three nighttime meetings after finishing my work in the office. Several months went by and nothing seemed to be changing, in fact I had to have shock therapy. Then another rather quick downturn of depression struck me. As usual, I called my psychiatrist at Duke and had him schedule me for another shock treatment the next morning. I had received a treatment only about six or seven weeks before. This time (about eight months after my brain surgery) I called Tommy and went up to the Mission and asked him to pray for me. It was the first time I'd asked him to do so. Never had I started down this steep incline to grim hopeless depression and had it lifted by anything other than a shock treatment. I didn't know what Tommy said but he prayed for me, and then I went back to my office practice. I didn't feel anything at all. When I finally got home a few hours later, I told Lou that I wasn't any better and that I had made arrangements to leave my practice for a day and go up to Duke Hospital the next morning for another shock treatment.

D. The Healing.

It was about three hours after the prayer while at home for lunch when I remarked, "My gosh, Lou, I think I might be getting a little better." I thought, "Maybe I won't have to have a shock treatment." Fifteen minutes later I had absolutely no symptoms of depression whatsoever! This kind of rapid recovery had never happened before! But just then a negative accusing voice, with which I was to become familiar, asked me, "What makes you think this will last?" Well, it did last, and each day and week that passed confirmed my healing, while that voice kept denying it. Finally, it hit me that God had totally healed me. Since the day Tommy prayed for me, I have never had clinical depression! "Healed! Praise God!" I had received a miracle that I'd hoped for but never really expected. "Thank you, Lord Jesus!" The devil had kept telling me it couldn't last, but now there was no denying it! "Thank you, Lord!" Jesus did for me in three hours what medicine could not do in twenty-one years. I called Duke and canceled the treatment.

As a patient I was thrilled. As a physician I was very impressed with this new therapy from Jesus Christ for this wasn't suppose to happen. It was totally unscientific and therefore, "impossible." My reasoning was, "this is the supernatural and I'm too intelligent to believe in that stuff!" I thought, "But I can't deny it, I don't want to deny my healing because it is so wonderful! So real! How can it be? How amazing, how utterly impossible!"

"Could Tommy have supplied the faith that I didn't have? This is too wild! Is medicine wrong and does healing through Jesus really occur? Of course, it's wrong! Of course it occurs! I am living proof of it! This is crazy! It's against everything I was brought up to believe and against all of my years of schooling and medical experience. Miracle healing? It doesn't make sense. I never saw a case of it in my life that I thought was real. But here I am, healed, after twenty-one years of hell. Medicine and science rejects the notion that God heals. But I am healed and they are wrong, dead wrong!"

For Dr. Hood and others who have suffered through mental illness such as panic disorder, bipolar, OCD, and others; I hope God has a special place in paradise reserved for them. They have already had a trip through hell on the back of a haunting malady.

CHAPTER SIX
LIFE IS —TRAGEDY, COURAGE, AND LOVE

$$\backsim\!o\!\backsim$$

T ragedies are nothing unusual. We hear of them almost every day. There are big ones and little ones, but even little ones can be devastating to the persons involved.

Some of the biggest headliners involve airplanes, varying in size from small single engine ones to commercial airlines.

And coal mine deaths, even though they have decreased greatly over the last few decades, still occur now and then.

Building collapses are also events that result in tragedy, causing deaths that sometime number in the hundreds.

Nature, of course, is the biggest producer of calamities. It's capable of killing people by the thousands through earthquakes, hurricanes, and other freaks of nature. Even our space program has provided us with a number of tragedies.

So, why have I chosen a tragedy involving such a small number of people, to represent the book's tragic side of life? Because, to Eleanor, the events depicted could hardly have been more devastating.

This narrative tells of a gracious lady who suffered a family tragedy after she had reached retirement age. It was of such magnitude that some people in her situation might have withdrawn from society and spent their time grieving over their loss.

She chose, however, not to do that, she wanted more of real life so she could assist the living by helping more children to learn more, by visiting the sick and lonely and by helping in church work and serving God.

She accomplished all these things, plus more, after returning to her roots, where she enjoys life tremendously at age 81.

I have known her closely for more than sixty years-and the events I have described in this section are all actual.

I can best describe it as an account of courage, tragedy and overwhelming love.

An abbreviated version of this account was included in "They Didn't Bring Ice on Sunday."

Eleanor

Just fourteen months after William E. Phillips and Mabel E. Griffin were married they were blessed with their first child. The date was January 24th in the year 1925, when Mary Eleanor Phillips arrived on the scene. She was a mighty pretty baby, but she was bald-so much so that they covered her pate when snapshots were made. After a couple of years, though, hair appeared. It was black, curly and as beautiful as could be-no more need to cover the dome when pictures were taken.

Eleanor was born with a few more smarts than most of us, enabling her to enter first grade of public school at age five. School was in the town of Trenton, eight miles away, which necessitated a school bus ride daily.

Her parents were lifelong farmers of Jones County, being owners of a moderate size farm, and that meant the money crop was tobacco. It also meant that at age of ten or twelve, the family children were expected to work in tobacco during harvest time. This included Eleanor Phillips, who became a "hander". She bunched up about four green leaves at the time and handed them to another person, known as a "looper", who then tied them onto a tobacco stick with tobacco twine. In addition to that, she also helped with preparation of meals.

At the end of the harvesting period it was usually time to return to school, where Eleanor was an excellent student, as well as a basketball player at Trenton High School. At age sixteen she graduated as class valedictorian. She had also been elected May Queen.

When she entered East Carolina Teachers College in Greenville, she pursued her dream of becoming a school teacher by electing education as her major, with special interest in Home Economics. She became somewhat of an expert in cooking and sewing-talents she still possesses. She and younger sister, Annie, looked forward to weekends away from college when her daddy, or another parent in the neighborhood, would pick them up at school and drive them home on Fridays and take them back on Sundays. There were times, for convenience sake, the girls would take a bus from E.C.T.C. to Kinston, where they would be picked up at the bus station by someone from home. A one-way ticket could be purchased at a cost of sixty-nine cents.

In the City of Greenville at that time there was an intersection referred to as "five-points". A name such as that naturally denotes confusion to non-residents-and it did to Mr. Phillips on one occasion-when he had picked up the girls and pointed his car in the direction of Kinston. When he reached the aforementioned intersection, he exited into the wrong lane, and there happened to be a cop standing right there. He put his hand up and motioned Mr. Phillips to stop the car. One could tell the law enforcement person was agitated-probably asking himself; "I wonder where this guy thinks he's going."

Now, let me tell you a little something about Jones County at that time. It was one of the poorer counties in the area. It was largely underdeveloped, its largest town being Trenton, which was not much more than a big intersection. It also consisted of very flat land and easily flooded when pounded by heavy thunderstorms. Crop areas were said to be inferior to some surrounding counties. All of those conditions resulted in the fact residents of the county were not held in highest esteem by those in wealthier counties, warranted, or not.

When the uniformed gentleman stopped Mr. Phillips, he began asking some nondescript questions in a belittling manner. He finally asked Mr. Phillips where he was from, who answered with the words, "Jones County". It's no wonder the traffic cop told him, "If that's where you're from-get on back down there!"

*   *   *

During her high school and college years Eleanor, having grown to be a real beauty, dated a number of boys, none of which she became serious with. She had her eyes set on a certain young man with hair as black as hers.

Inasmuch as she wanted only him, she more or less put a ban on dating others, but nothing of a matrimonial nature materialized until World War II. That was a time in which Louis Smith, like millions more, served his country as a U.S. Marine in the Pacific Theater of Operations. He was engaged in the deadly game of island hopping-resulting in a wound for which he received the Purple Heart.

After his military discharge, Louis decided to make a career as a North Carolina Highway Patrolman. Another thing he decided to do was to get serious with the teacher, if it was her husband he wanted to be.

Activity revved up in the dating game and they both decided they wanted the same name. Did he catch her or did she catch him? It didn't really matter-they soon became man and wife.

The trooper's first assignment was to a little town named Shallotte, an out of the way place between Wilmington, N.C. and the South Carolina border. That must have been a place where they sent rookie patrolman for their first tour of duty in order to determine if they really wanted to make the Patrol their career. Back then it could have been referred to as a "jumping off" place. If so, he passed the test assignment-he was transferred to Wilmington the very next year.

Assuming he would remain in Wilmington for several years, the couple purchased a home and settled in for what would be a sixteen year stint. The city was-and still is-considered one of the better places to live in the State of North Carolina. It has several nice ocean beaches nearby, which afford ample space for sun worshippers to lie and soak in those cancer-causing solar rays.

Salt water fishing spots are in abundance in the Atlantic and its tributaries. On the other side of the city fresh water fishermen can find rivers or creeks in which to wet a line. For the Smiths it was also a great place to rear two daughters.

The couple attempted for a number of years to plant people seed that would germinate-but without success-so they finally adopted Rosemary as a baby. As often happens, six years later germination did occur and Betty Lou was the result.

Things went well on the Tar Heel coast and the Smith family made many friends. They hoped to retire right there as patrolman and school teacher, but it wasn't to be. The commander's edict was, "Louis, we need you in Goldsboro"-and that was a command. So, the four of them moved to the Wayne County city and bought a house on a street named-would you believe-Elanor? Her name without the second "E".

Louis was elevated to rank of sergeant and Eleanor settled in at a nearby public school as social studies teacher.

Rosemary and Betty Lou became students in nearby schools. Life was really bright for the Smith family and their home became a gathering place frequently for family get togethers. Their home was the most convenient for the remainder of the Phillips clan to meet-and the Smith hospitality was always at a high level.

Rosemary met her future husband at Atlantic Christian College and they soon were married.

Life progressed and Betty Lou entered the University of North Carolina. In addition to golf, Ole Sarge pursued a hobby of wood-working and constructed a shop in his back yard to further his endeavor. He became proficient and began making tables, chests, armoires, pie chests and other woodwork pieces. He made two or three odd pieces for me. His work was extremely good. His last piece would be a beautiful dining table to be placed in a new addition to their house.

Smitty retired after pulling his thirty years on the highways of North Carolina, allowing him to chase that little white ball more often-occasionally with me-and he spent more time in his shop.

Eleanor, after serving a term of thirty one years as public servant, joined Louis in retirement. She had time to sew, cook, perform church work and help others. Life still seemed good.

Things Gone Awry

Except for Louis taking blood pressure pills, the family was in generally good health, but in the fall of 1982 Louis began having back pains. One day after a round of golf he stopped by his doctor's office to be checked. As soon as he lay on his back on the doctor's table, the doc told him he could feel what appeared to be a tumor in his abdominal area. He was sent to Duke Hospital and it was there that a diagnosis of Non-Hodgkin's Lymphoma was rendered in January 1983.

This shattered the world of serenity the family had so recently entered. From that day their lives would be altered forever. That is what cancer can do to people.

Many years ago the word "cancer' was almost taboo. It struck fear in every family it attacked and every victim's family made an attempt to hide it from the public. Very little was known about the disease, except it was deadly and treatment was limited. Thankfully, by the time Louis was diagnosed, effective treatment was available. In fact, he was told by his physician that, if he had to contract cancer, he had chosen the right kind. He would be given standard chemo-therapy treatment and would probably live for years.

Dosage prescribed was to be administered once weekly; first at Duke and later at a clinic in Wilson.

Chemotherapy has saved many lives, of course, but in many cases there is a price to pay for this. In the case of Louis Smith in 1983 and 1984 his first side effect was loss of hair, as is the case in most situations. I think he took it in stride and in due course his hair re-grew, as coal black as ever. When I jokingly mentioned this to him one day his response was, "Well, it was black when it left me and it returned the same color-why shouldn't it?"

During the course of treatment his leg muscles were adversely affected. There were times when he had to crawl in order to get from his chair to the sofa in the den. He also developed blood clots, shingles, and diarrhea-and finally some heart trouble appeared. He also had a kidney removed during this time when it was discovered it wasn't functioning-and probably had not done so for years.

After taking continuous treatment for almost two years, his condition improved, but he was not in complete remission-even though he had become able to resume some of his everyday activities.

Real Tragedy

Having transferred from UNC to Appalachian State College in Boone, NC earlier, Betty was set for graduation in December 1984. There she would receive her diploma with honors. She had majored in Art Marketing and had done internship at the Folk Art Center in Asheville, NC, for the last phase of her education. It was there where she met and fell in love with Scott, an employee of the Center. It wasn't long before they became engaged-two fine young people deeply in love.

A few days prior to graduation, Betty wasn't feeling well and decided to visit the school's infirmary. An x-ray was taken, after which she was told she appeared to have "walking pneumonia". At home she was taken to the family doctor in Goldsboro, who agreed with that conclusion; however, she was having shortness of breath, so he referred her to a pulmonary specialist in Goldsboro. He found that one lung was completely enclosed in fluid. In February a decision was made to take her to memorial Hospital in Chapel Hill. Doctors there had to remove part of a rib in order to perform a biopsy. Memorial is a teaching hospital and as many as twelve doctors became involved in examining the lab report and other extensive tests. From those tests a diagnosis was arrived.

At that time there were said to be 37 strains of Non-Hodgkin's Lymphoma. After doctors secured her father's records, they came to the conclusion that Betty Lou and Louis were suffering from the very same strain. What an extraordinary occurrence.

There are times in life, for some people, when they have to reach deep down inside themselves and grasp every fiber of strength, fortitude and faith that's stored up in them. This had become that time for the Louis Smith family. Father and daughter would be treated for the same type cancer at the same time.

She received the same treatment he had received, resulting in the loss of her beautiful long black hair. It had set her apart from most girls and made her very attractive. When that happened she refused to wear a wig; instead, she fashioned a bandana around her head that served the purpose until Eleanor, being the seamstress she was, devised a turban. She made one to match each outfit.

Betty persevered through treatments and Scott would visit the Smith residence on weekends. In this way they could be together as much as possible.

He went with her one Sunday to the Phillips farm for a family gathering and meal, at which I was present.

After the meal, the two of them stole away and walked to the fish pond in the field back of the house to have some time alone. I could only imagine what they talked about as I saw them walk slowly away, hand in hand, two of God's beautiful young children facing a monumental problem. I doubt either of them realized the severity of it at the time.

I can suppose she was telling Scott about the wedding dress on which her parents had made a deposit at a store in Wilson-and other aspects of their forthcoming ceremony. Maybe even about job hunting for the two of them after her recovery and, who knows, maybe the possibility of children-and how many. Maybe they talked about the wedding band they had picked out.

As days passed into weeks and weeks into months, doctors realized the treatments being administered were not having the desired effect. Not only had she not gone into remission-her condition was not improving. Instead, it was gradually deteriorating. This resulted in her admission to Memorial Hospital again.

The situation had reached a critical stage and things had not come together in Chapel Hill as hoped for, despite trying every procedure doctors could come up with. She was then transferred to Duke Hospital for whatever they could do on an experimental basis.

Eleanor says she has never forgotten seeing personnel who worked on Betty Lou don protective clothing from head to foot. This was to protect them against a possible drop of the poisonous medication they were dripping directly into her daughter's body. As a last resort, a bone marrow transplant was performed, using her own marrow.

On Sunday, October 6, Louis suffered a heart attack while attending church service in Goldsboro. The rescue squad was called and they immediately took him to Wayne Memorial Hospital in the same city.

Shortly afterward, while riding in a car with Eleanor, I heard her make this remark during a conversation concerning her predicament; "I know one thing, if Betty Lou Smith dies, Louis Smith will die." The transplant didn't work.

Eleanor had her hands full with a husband in a hospital in Goldsboro suffering with a heart attack-and a twenty-three year old daughter in worse condition in Durham. Impossible to be in both places at the same time. Scott, that wonderful young man whom his fiancée dearly loved, had taken leave from his job when things became critical. He was in constant presence at the hospital and in her room helping his "girl".

On October 10, 1985, four days after her father suffered his heart attack, this young girl in the prime of her life, passed away-just as beautiful on the inside as on the outside.

The day before, when Rosemary was sitting with her, Betty Lou had said to her, "Rosemary, isn't that music beautiful?" "What music Betty Lou?" "That music, it's beautiful, don't you hear it?"

Another member of the family overheard her repeating something similar to an incantation, with the word "father" being spoken frequently. Never in her lifetime had she called Louis "father".

Louis and Eleanor had lost a daughter. Rosemary had lost a sister. Mike and Betsy had lost a granddaughter-and God had added a second Phillips angel to his chorus.

Eleanor asked me to call Louis's doctor and ask him if he thought she should tell Louis about his daughter's death. His advice was not to do so-his heart might not take it. Eleanor felt that Betty Lou should not be buried without her daddy's knowledge, so on Sunday morning prior to the afternoon funeral she called Dr. Bennett and requested he inform Louis of the event. He did so in the presence of Louis's brother, Elza, and wife, Margaret.

When we sit down with family and consume a good meal, it's usually a joyful occasion, but not that Sunday noon. I had become quite an emotional person through the entire ordeal-and I had diffi-culty properly giving thanks for the meal.

The service that afternoon was sad, of course. Many people refer to funerals as celebrations of the lives of the deceased. On this occa-sion I found myself unable to have that feeling.

After the funeral procession had traveled about forty miles, the service was completed in the Phillips family cemetery in Jones County.

Just six days after the death of Betty Lou Smith, Eleanor's predic-tion became a reality-Louis Smith died. His heart simply could not withstand the shock. His death occurred October 16, at the age of 62.

Another casket, another procession and another burial at the same site from which the funeral tent had not even been removed. A dedicated father and husband had been lost.

I do not possess the ability to express in words my feeling of condolence in a tragedy such as this. Thankfully, some others do- and Eleanor received a number of them. Below are two such expressions that show what impact Betty Lou Smith had on the lives of two people who knew her well. The first is from a professor at Appalachian State University and the second from an associate of Folk Art Center, under whom she did her internship.

To the parents of Betty Lou Smith:

I have recently learned of the death of your daughter. I was deeply saddened that the life of such a fine young woman has ended. Betty was liked by everybody who knew her, faculty and students alike. She completed two classes with me, one Studio in Fibers and one in Art History entitled Women Artists. In both courses she performed very well, but in the latter, one memory in particular stands out. When she presented her research paper on Coca Chanel, she came dressed as the famous designer. "Chanel suite", "pearls", "white gloves", etc. She charmed the entire class.

As a mother of two daughters my heart goes out to you. As a professor of hers my heart also goes out to you and all those people that had not met her yet or been influenced by her.

Dear Mrs. Smith

I have been wanting to write you for several weeks now, but didn't know exactly what to say. The hurt and pain you have experienced during the last year and especially the last month is certainly immeasurable. And I just want you to know that I have been praying for you and will continue to do so-as well as your daughter and grandchildren.

Memories are such treasures! And those I have of Betty Lou are exactly that-golden treasures. She was one of the nicest and most thoughtful young ladies I've ever met and had the opportunity to work with. I loved her dearly and I've looked forward to the day I will see her again in her beauty and sweetness that I will always remember. When I think how much we all loved Betty and wanted her to stay with us, I can't help but think how much more the Lord loved her and wanted her home with Him. To know that she is free of pain and beautiful again helps me to let her go, but I must admit that her earthly death has hurt me as much as if she were a part of my family. She and Scott were and are very dear to all of us at the office.

We had the pleasure of watching their love for one another blossom and mature, and we will always love them.

As a mother of two I simply can't honestly imagine what you must be going through losing both your daughter and husband so closely together. I pray that the Lord will supply your every need and carry you through this sad time.

Please know that I am available if you need anything-just call the office or my home any time.

May God's love and strength be with you.

*   *   *

We humans have various ways in which to express our thanks, our sympathy, our congratulations, our condolences, our happiness, our sorrow or our love to one another.

A few years back there was a lady in our church congregation who kept records of the birth dates of every member of the church-and she made a point of calling each on that date to wish them a "Happy Birthday". Annie and I have certainly missed her calls since she passed away.

Some people choose to send birthday cards. This is especially true of siblings, so Annie can expect to get a handful every birthday.

When we bestow a wedding gift to a newly married couple, we more or less expect to receive a "thank you" note in return. Sometimes we get one-sometimes we don't.

When someone unexpectedly does something nice for us, we can pick up the telephone and thank them personally or we can mail a short note.

Our sympathy is expressed to survivors of lost loved ones through mailing of condolence cards purchased at card shops.

Love for another is often expressed by a shoulder hug or a kiss.

Have you ever thought about how you would go about expressing love to someone who had spent a lifetime caring for you in every way? Someone who suffered the throes of childbirth pain in order to bring you into this world? Someone who nursed you, fed you, and rocked you to sleep as an infant? Somebody who picked you up gently and calmed you when you stumbled and bumped your head? Someone who helped you with homework when you needed it? Someone who watched you grow up day by day and who helped you in your transition from a girl to a young lady? Someone with whom you had rapport that only the two of you understood? Someone who, in the last weeks of your life, had shown more love for you than you ever thought possible? Someone who would have gladly given her life to save yours, had that been possible?

How would you say, "Good-bye, I love you" to someone who had spent a lifetime lavishing you with affection?

Betty Lou Smith had her inimitable way of doing just that-a way that never would have crossed the minds of most of us.

Near the end, when Betty realized her situation had reached a critical stage, she chose three pages from a simple note pad as the method by which she would use to glorify her mother. Those pages were 6 x 9 inches, about the size of the page you are now reading. Each note was written on a different date. The purpose of each was to extol her mother and to show gratitude for her unceasing graciousness. Each one was put in an out of sight place where nobody but Eleanor would find it, and a place where she knew her mother would forage almost daily.

The first was found by Eleanor in her jewelry box. The second was found in her dresser drawer, both being found within a day or two. The third, and last, was written just before Betty was to leave the house for the last time-a journey to Duke Hospital-a trip from which she would not return. The last note would not be discovered for several weeks. This was due to the fast pace of events leading up to Betty's demise, plus the many details to be attended to prior to and after two funerals. When all those details had been taken care of, Eleanor found the third note in her shoe box full of buttons. It's ironic this love note was found in a container through which Eleanor had rifled so many times in the past, looking for a just right button to fashion something for Betty Lou. This one page, consisting of 108 words, would be the last written correspondence from daughter to mother. It was especially endearing and something Eleanor had shared with no one-until now. The contents of which follow:

Dear Mama,

I love you. It's so hard for those three little words to really express how I feel for you. I believe you're an angel God has sent-my guardian angel. You've been there for me to talk to, cry to, laugh with. You've made me a sandwich when I didn't feel like moving. You've helped me to stay busy so I wouldn't eat myself up with worry. You've hugged me when I needed it most. The list could go on for years.

You've done all that could possibly be done-you've been perfect. I love you-you're my best friend, my mother, and my strength.

Betty Lou

Yes, true love is a many splendored thing.

*   *   *

It's tragedy enough to lose just one member of a person's immediate family. To lose a spouse and child in this manner and in such a short period of time must be devastating. It takes a sturdy person to absorb such shock and sorrow-and then have the fortitude to build a new life and adjust to a new family environment. Such a person was Eleanor Smith.

I attempted to assist her in a few minor details that had to be taken care of shortly after the deaths. So did other members of her family, but by and large, she made the transition herself.

One of the first decisions she made was to ask Rosemary and family to move in with her for a period of time. She didn't want to face the loneliness that must be overwhelming when, all of a sudden, you find yourself all alone in your home; nobody to talk to across the kitchen table; nobody to fix that leaking faucet; nobody to push a chair back and say, "Mom, that spaghetti was delicious." There would be nobody to lean on at the end of a day in which everything seemed to go wrong; nobody to peck you on the cheek and say, "I love you"; nobody to give you that feeling of security lying beside you in bed at night; nor hear footsteps on a threshold at the end of a work day.

Having her daughter's family in the same house helped a great deal in putting the past behind her and preparing for the future.

A few years later, after her abbreviated family had moved out, she had a desire to return to her roots in Jones County and be near two of her brothers, Horace and Don, who still lived on the home place.

Siblings were concerned that she might not be making the right decision. After all, she had lived in Goldsboro all those years-her friends were there, her church was there. Would she be happy leaving all that and returning to a farming area in one of the poorer counties of the state? She ignored them all-she knew how she would fare.

She put her house on the market and immediately made arrangements to have a pre-fabricated house constructed by a firm in Beulaville, NC. Fortunately, her Goldsboro home sold about the same time the new house was finished. It was hauled in one piece on a huge tractor-trailer and set up on a lot owned by brother Horace-just across the highway from his home.

This proved to be a great move for her, allowing her to renew old friendships and gain new ones. It also meant two close brothers would be only a stone's throw away should help be needed.

* * *

Her life has been full at Highway 58 North-driving her Skylark back and forth to visit sick friends, volunteer teach, attend church, attend quilting classes and enjoy fellowship with the "Forever Young Club". She has recently completed classes at Barton College on Saturdays in order to obtain a degree in ministerial studies from the school's Lay Academy. She received her first degree at age 20 and a second one at age 80.

Yes, she has had more than her share of tragedy, which she will never forget, but she still has chosen to thank God for what she does have. This includes a daughter and two grandchildren, two sisters (one of which is my wife) and three brothers-as well as a host of friends.

Someone once said,"If life gives you a lemon, make lemonade." Mary Eleanor Phillips Smith has squeezed every drop.

She was recently given a reception in honor of her 80th birthday. I wrote a rather lengthy tribute in celebration of her life, the last few sentences of which follow:

"You still have people to love and be loved in return, and still a little energy at eighty to burn. Please keep on doing what you do so well-the things that make life for many so swell.

Keep making your home for siblings a motel. Keep feeding the preacher and others as well. Keep taking food to the sick you know and counseling them when spirits are low.

There's a place in heaven for people like you-who, for others, have a tendency to do and do. If, when life ebbs, you get there first-please save a place for the rest of us.

Happy 80th Eleanor-we wish you more."

CHAPTER SEVEN
LIFE IS —ENDURANCE

❦

﹎

M ost of us, if we have a choice between life and death, will choose life. If we believe in the healing power of God, we will go to Him in times of critical illness and ask for an extension of it. Sometimes we attempt to barter with Him, promising all the good things we will do, if He will just let us live a little longer on this earth.

I recently saw a news flash announcing the discovery of a new drug. It had the potential to extend life two months longer in certain cancer patients than other drugs now on the market. Imagine that-a drug that will give us two more months of life. It seems that drugs now available will give patients nine months of life after diagnosis, whereas, the new one will promise eleven months. No pronounce-ment was made concerning the projected cost of the new one when approved by the FDA. I suspect it will be phenomenal. Even so, most patients would jump at the opportunity to buy sixty days of life sustaining breath, regardless of the poor quality of life that might have to be endured. I suppose it's only human nature to want to hang onto every thread of life as long as possible.

I had a friend who was diagnosed with cancer years ago and it wasn't discovered until it was in an advanced stage. It necessitated massive doses of chemotherapy-plus surgery. It was not long before he was bedridden at home. He gradually deteriorated, despite receiving chemotherapy on a regular schedule.

When it became obvious treatments were not effective, and his cancer was in a terminal stage, his medical doctor said to him, "Jim, there is nothing more I can do for you. Why don't you just discontinue treatments and try to enjoy what life you have left at home with the family?"

Another doctor, who apparently had a different philosophy regarding life, encouraged Jim to do the opposite-he should continue treatments as long as there was a shred of life left. Jim heeded the second doctor's advice and continued treatments. A short time later his life on earth ceased. He was willing to endure the horrible ill effects of treatment in order to have more life.

Now, let's look at the other side of the coin. I knew a gracious lady who, in her late seventies, was diagnosed with colon cancer, resulting in surgery to remove the damaged portion. Surgery was successful and she had several good years before cancer returned in her late eighties. After a few days in the hospital, doctors advised her that her condition was critical, but she could gain a few more months of life with more surgery and chemotherapy. Her response was, "No, I don't want anymore treatment. I have had a good life and have made my peace with God. I am ready to go." That night she died peacefully, shortly after having been told another grand-child had just been born. She chose not to endure the side effects she knew would invade her-for just a little more of life.

I was faced with a critical decision, myself, at age 77 and had to make a decision when I was diagnosed with prostate cancer. In the past I had heard that if a man was diagnosed with the disease past age 70, he would probably be better off doing nothing about it-that he would probably die of something else before the cancer would kill him and he would live a better lifestyle.

When the biopsy showed the extent in which the malignancy had progressed, I decided to go through 39 sessions of radiation and simply endure the consequences.

*   *   *

There are times when a patient will choose death if he or she suffers severe pain long enough.

Many years ago I enrolled in a Dale Carnegie public speaking course in which we had to recite a true experience we had endured sometime in our life span. It seems odd that I would remember any specific narrative other than my own-since that must have been about 1958-but I do recall one. One of the guys from out of town told of a memorable event involving his family. His dad had been suffering from cancer for several years and it was becoming very painful. When time came that death appeared imminent, all his children visited the same day and gathered in the room in which he had been bedridden for weeks.

During some point in their conversation his dad spoke these words: "When you children go to bed tonight, don't ask God to prolong my life, just ask Him to take it. I'm so tired." He died before daybreak.

E. Walker

A few days ago I lost a great friend of many years who was seventy-six, twenty years after he was diagnosed with Parkinson 's disease.

E. Walker Sugg was born in Greene County, just outside Snow Hill, NC, on a farm owned by his family. He attended public schools, after which he attended North Carolina State College-majoring in Dairy Manufacturing. That enabled him to secure a job with Carolina Dairies in Kinston, just fifteen miles from home. The firm engaged in bottling milk and later in the manufacture of ice cream. That job would turn out to be a lifetime career. During that time he and the owner, Merle Edwards, would develop a personal and business relationship that would last a lifetime. Some would say Merle treated Walker almost like a son. For the last twenty years of his employment, Walker's position at the firm was as general manager.

He and I attended Gordon Street Christian Church in our early years, but we didn't become close friends until we became charter members of Northwest Christian Church in 1956. At that time the new church was very close knit and it became easy to develop compatible groups. From that period a closeness between the Rouse family and Sugg family occurred.

I was a few years older than Walker but we both married in the same year-1947. He married Mary Ann Moore and I married Annie Phillips. We both became fathers of two children each, a son and daughter.

Later in life he and I became partners in a golf foursome that lasted many years-until he decided to pull out due to Parkinson's.

During that relationship we were fortunate enough to be able to take golf trips on a number of occasions. The foursome consisted of Walker, Carlton Oliver, Leslie Davis and myself. Our wives usually went along: Mary Ann, Pearl Oliver, Hazel Davis, and Annie. We played courses from Orlando, Fla., to Burlington, Vermont-and many in between. On those trips Leslie and I were partners, but on our local course in weekly matches Walker and I partnered.

I recall an incident from one of our trips to Disney World-where we eventually played all four courses. Each detail is etched in my mind even today, and I'm still reminded of it occasionally by the other guys.

I was regarded as a skinny person until I reached my forties; in fact, I weighed only 129 pounds when drafted into military service in 1943. I weighed 145 when discharged 33 months later. A few years ago I discovered food was good, especially when I found something I liked. I ascended to 165.

The winter prior to this particular trip I found a lot of stuff I liked and added about 15 pounds, making my weight approach 180. That was an unheard of weight for me. I vowed to bring it down to an acceptable level of 165 before trip time arrived. I knocked off all sweets and when we departed Kinston for Orlando I was down to 165. I was starving for sweets.

After the first round of golf we stopped at a dairy bar which could produce the most beautiful banana splits I had ever laid my eyes upon. They were big-and expensive. My mouth was watering. I could just see myself diving into that big mess of ice cream piled on top of that banana, topped with walnuts. I was ready to order that delectable looking monstrosity-then Annie spoke. "Ray, I want some, too, but I certainly can't eat a whole one. You don't need a whole one, yourself. Why don't we order just one and split the split? You can start at one end and I'll start at the other. We'll meet in the middle."

I pondered that statement for just a moment and came to the conclusion it would be satisfactory with me. After all, my mouth was bigger than her mouth, my stomach was bigger than her stomach and I knew I was hungrier than she. I figured I would come out ahead in the projected scenario. "Give us one banana split-with two spoons."

When that gorgeous piece of art was placed in front of us, instead of waiting for somebody to say "go", I plunged my spoon into the first scoop of chocolate I saw. I didn't wait to savor the taste-I just devoured the chocolate and headed for the pile of vanilla. The entire event didn't take long-and one thing you can be assured of-we didn't meet in the middle!

Another event that stands out in my mind involving Walker occurred shortly after the Branson, Missouri, attractions came into being. The Rouses, Davises, and Suggs rented a seven passenger van and I was elected chauffeur and tour guide. We headed for Branson.

When we left Kinston we loaded lots of foodstuff. We had cookies, chips, drinks, and fruit-but no refuse bag. Late in the day I asked for an apple to be passed to me to eat while driving in a non-congested area. I ate it to the core, and then asked someone to drop it in the trash bag. I was advised there was no such thing aboard-so I ate the remainder-core, seed, stem and whatever.

Our first stop was in Asheville, NC, where we stopped and toured the magnificent Grove Park Inn about noontime. We then resumed our journey westward on I-40 and spent the night some distance east of Nashville, Tenn. Next day we stopped in Memphis to tour Graceland, and spent that night somewhere west of there. Next day we arrived in Branson, where things were really jumping. We stayed there two days and three nights-or was it three days and two nights? At any rate, the place met our expectations and shows were enjoyed by all.

After leaving Branson we caught a tip of Oklahoma, and then headed for Kansas City, where we toured the Harry Truman sites. We stopped next for a short time at the Arch in St. Louis-then to all the Abe Lincoln sites in Illinois, Indiana and Kentucky. When we arrived back home we all agreed a great time was had by all-and our billfolds were somewhat thinner.

*   *   *

When Walker was told he had Parkinson's, he knew what he was up against. He was aware that it was an illness that would not take him away anytime soon. He also knew it would eventually become a disabler-maybe something even worse than death. He was told that with the right medication, he could have some years of good quality life. He could still enjoy Mary Ann and Emmett and Ann and grandchildren-plus golf.

Drugs for Parkinson's, as is the case for many other drugs, were very expensive from the beginning. They became even more so over the years as newer medicines became available on a rather regular basis. Each new year brought higher bills. But Walker was still a relatively young man who wanted to live life to its fullest as long as he could. He didn't fuss nor fret over the cost.

He maintained some proficiency in golf for a few short years, but the illness finally manifested itself on Walker's scorecard. He remained a good putter but his distance off the tee and fairways steadily declined. He realized his competitiveness was fleeting, so he withdrew from the foursome and was replaced by Myron Hill.

Walker and Mary Ann had a place at Kennels Beach, about an hour drive from Kinston, and they increased the time they spent there. They stayed at their home in Kinston during winter months only. It was at the river that he enjoyed his last few years fishing and boating, often accompanied by his children and grandkids. His children presented him with a new golf cart which he enjoyed driving around the beach area.

As Parkinson's really began taking its toll, he became confined to a wheel chair and his speech became somewhat muted. His volume decreased and it was difficult for those of us outside the family to converse with him.

As much as Walker loved life-for the last few years-he wanted to die, but death wouldn't come. There were times he would simply pass out and crumble to the floor. He requested Mary Ann not to call a doctor nor dial 911 in those situations. He was fully aware his usefulness in this life had been voided and he was ready to meet life waiting for him in paradise in the company of his Lord.

About three years before the end Mary Ann was fortunate to find Maddie, that wonderful angel, to become Walker's caretaker. She cared for him as if he were her dad. They fell in love with each other and the love affair lasted until March 14, 2005.

Maddie had a routine of going to the house at 9 a.m., bathing him and putting him in a lounge chair for the day-and would care for him until days end. She would then leave and go to her own home, but would return to the Sugg house at 9 p.m. and put him to bed.

On that fateful morning she arrived at her usual time and prepared to give him his daily bath. As she lifted him she asked how he felt and he answered in a voice barely audible, "good". Then his body became limp. At first Maddie and Mary Ann wondered if this might be just another passing out spell, but then Maddie perceived a slight gutteral sound. She recognized it as a death rattle. She knew Walker had drawn his last breath. At long last his prayers of several years duration, asking for death to occur, had been answered.

At that moment Mary Ann lost a faithful husband, Ann and Emmett lost a great father, Kimberly, Lindsay, and Eric lost a wonderful grandfather-and heaven's population increased by one.

I can truthfully say I have not personally known a better man than Emmett Walker Sugg. He was a first class gentleman and a genuine Christian. I don't recall him uttering a word of profanity in my presence, nor did I ever see him truly angry. Neither did I ever hear him complain of his illness-nor he never questioned the reason for it by asking, "Why me, Lord?"

I don't have the wherewithal to truly express the impact this man had on his family and others around him, but his daughter, Ann, did have. She exhibited that ability by composing a beautiful poem which was printed on the backside of the order of service bulletins. They were handed out to the many friends and relatives who attended the memorial service at Northwest Christian Church in Kinston at 2 p.m., March 16, 2005. The poem is shown below.

To Walker...

What have I done with my life? said he.
No fame or glory for all the world to see,
No famous buildings bear my name,
When I leave this earth all will be the same.

How could you not realize; how could you not know
That life will be measured by the seeds of kindness you
sow.
The measure of a man is not gauged by fame or acclaim
But by the amount of love you spread in Christ Jesus'
name.

You lived your whole life by the examples He set;

A life that well lived leaves no room for regret.

With charity and grace you've lived out your days

Earning our respect, undying love, and praise.

You've fought the good fight, the battle you've won,

You can rest with the Lord for your work here is done.

We've been blessed by your honesty, goodness and love

For your fine example we thank the Lord up above.

More important than landmarks, more precious than gold

Your sweet, sweet spirit passes down as your story is told.

With courage, good values, and all that is true,

We'll let your light shine in all that we do.

Ann Sugg Leary

"Let your light so shine before men, that they may see your good works and give glory to your Father who is in heaven."

Matthew 5:16

Yes, Walker Sugg endured the effects of Parkinson's disease for twenty years before he succumbed to that dreadful illness.

CHAPTER EIGHT
LIFE IS—A POTPOURRI

∞

I really like this section of the book. To me, that word potpourri has a simple definition: "lotza stuff". In other words, it gives me journalistic freedom to write about anything that comes to mind. I don't have to correlate anything I write here with other portions of the book. I don't have to worry about having too many peaks and valleys. I don't have to worry about putting you out on a tangent tether and having to bring you back in. I don't have to worry about sticking to a specific subject because there isn't one. You might say I'm just rambling around a bit and covering lots of stuff.

When striking up a conversation with someone you're not acquainted with, it's always acceptable to talk about the weather-so here goes.

This land of ours is so vast that the weather is never the same in all sections at the same time. Take our West Coast, for instance. It's noted for three facets of weather: earthquakes, fires, and mudslides. Earthquakes are the biggie. It is said that almost daily an earth rumble of some degree is felt in some part of the state. The populace doesn't seem to be concerned, however, and their love of the state is such that they are willing to take the risk of being hit by the "really big one" that is predicted to hit the area at some point in time.

Mudslides are not the menace earthquakes are, but they are capable of toppling dwellings of those who build too close to cliffs in order to have a close view of the pacific, or another body of water. Not a great number of lives are lost in the torrential rain season, but property damage can be heavy.

The other great menace to the golden state residents is that of forest fires which occur mainly in the southern half of the state. In our seven week cross-country trip in 1987, we traveled the scenic seventeen mile auto tour around Pebble Beach. A few hours after we left, a good portion of the area was left in ashes due to a forest fire. Damage was minimal compared to that sustained in the Los Angeles area every year during forest fire season. That problem is brought about to a great extent when residents leave densely populated urban areas to seek more desirable environs. They accomplish this by invading heavily wooded areas with beautiful vistas in outlying suburbs that become tinderboxes in dry seasons.

In the fall of 2003 a forest fire cost the lives of a number of people and destroyed more than 2,600 homes and blackened over 700,000 acres. Since this becomes almost an annual occurrence one would think residents would hesitate to build in the areas. But not so. One resident was interviewed who said his second house had just been destroyed-and he planned to rebuild in the same spot.

*   *   *

The weather in our Midwest seems to be changing a trifle. Over the last few years winters haven't been as harsh as they were when our daughter Cindy married and moved there almost twenty years ago.

They first lived in Appleton, Wisconsin, for a couple of years. They then moved north to the village of Denmark, which is about a dozen miles south of Green Bay, and they remained there for two years prior to moving to Monroe, Wisconsin, where they have remained.

Those first few winters were long and cold. It was nothing for temps to fall below zero. One winter Annie, Mike, and I flew to Madison to spend Christmas. It's only an hour away from Monroe. From the time we entered Wisconsin, after flying over Lake Michigan, I thought maybe the pilot had made a wrong reading and had taken us into Alaska air space. Every foot of earth was covered in a thick blanket of snow. Immediately after landing and prior to debarking, the pilot announced that when we left the plane we would be entering an atmosphere with a temperature of ten degrees below zero. Ed soon entered the terminal with an armful of heavy coats. He advised us the car heater was not working fully and we might need the heavy clothing in order to be comfortable during the ride to Monroe. On the way there we passed several lakes on which some hardy souls were ice fishing.

Evidence that temperatures are moderating somewhat proved itself about three months ago-when a father and daughter were drowned in a pond on which ice was too thin for ice skating and it caved in on them. Aside from cold temperatures, the Midwest is also a favorite target for tornados. Fierce storms pass through the area's "Tornado Alley" on a rather frequent basis.

I believe the Northeast section of our country has become home to our harshest winters. It isn't too unusual for the area to have two or three heavy snowfalls during a winter season. Just this year some places around New York had their deepest snow on record.

Dumb blond joke: This beautiful blonde became intrigued with ice fishing, so she read up on the sport in sport magazines and finally decided to try it.

She bought all the necessary equipment and on the next day off from work she got everything together and headed for a large area of thick ice. She unfolded her chair and made ready to cut a hole in the ice when, from the sky a voice boomed, "There are no fish under the ice!" She didn't question the command. She simply gathered her stuff and moved to another location.

She began to cut another hole and again the same voice: "You won't find fish under the ice." She was getting perturbed and moved to the other end.

She bent over once more to cut a hole. Again the same voice: "You won't find fish under the ice." She looked up at the sky and asked, "Is that you Lord?" "No. I'm manager of the hockey rink."

Now let's cover the Southeast, of which North Carolina is a part. Our nemesis is hurricanes. Thankfully, our state hasn't had the number or severity of these storms that Florida has. I hope we can continue to avoid all storms with the strength and magnitude of the late "Katrina".

*   *   *

When we built this house thirty years ago, Annie wanted one extra thing we hadn't planned on originally, a back porch. Just a small porch, one to which she could go and enjoy a cup of coffee, an area of about 10 x 10 feet. Instead of that, we decided on a 10 x 30 area, which we screened. Some years later we decided it would be more functional if it was enclosed, so we did it by utilizing sliding glass doors, which also have screens. It has worked out perfectly for us and is the most used area in the house except for the den. But it is still just a porch. It's neither a sun room nor a solarium, although some people refer to it as such.

After the last tax revaluation was completed we received the usual notification, along with an explanatory sheet telling us how they had arrived at the new value.

When I glimpsed the county's estimate of worth for our place of abode, I sat upright. Never in my sweetest dreams had I imagined being owner of a home with its value being as astronomical as the county folks had perceived our place to be. Surely a mistake had been made. I labored over the report, sheet by sheet, item by item. Then I spotted something that showed three story solarium"-$90,000. Whoa! Three story solarium? We didn't even have a one story solarium, just a one story porch. A porch is a porch, a porch is a porch, a porch is a porch-and ours is easily identifiable as such by simply looking at its clutter. After discovering the error it was easy enough to get corrected. Problem solved.

We can now use the space for almost anything except cooking, laundering, and bathing. We have wicker in one end which enables us to take naps, if so desired. We have two metal round tables in the other end-which become useful when we have clan gatherings. They can seat four each. We have also used it for showing slides to groups as large as twenty.

*   *   *

From this porch I'm going to walk you through a fringe hurricane so you might get some insight into the little inconveniences even a fringe one can cause, date: September 18, 2003.

The one I'm waiting for is not supposed to be a big blow. Being about fifty miles from nearest oceanic waters, we get only the fringe of most hurricanes that make land along the Carolina coasts. There have, however, been a few really big ones to hit us in past years.

The worst one I can recall was in 1954, when Hazel's eye moved directly over Kinston carrying winds of 150 mph. A few two-story buildings became one-story as it passed through our area. She was certainly no lady. We're not expecting any such destruction from Isabel.

There are some storms in which torrents of rain descend for hours on end, doing much more damage than the wind. Such a blow was Hurricane Floyd, which visited us in 1999-and flooded the eastern portion of the state.

That was one which we did not personally witness, because we were visiting our Wisconsin family at the time. We were keeping up with its movements through TV news and newspaper articles. They related events that were causing highways to become rivers.

The day after Floyd had passed; our return flight to Raleigh-Durham was delayed for 24 hours because planes were unable to land there.

When we arrived there the next day and were descending, I could hardly believe the amount of water we saw in low grounds surrounding the airport.

We then couldn't reach Kinston by auto on our usual route of highway 70, due to some stretches being flooded and having some bridges washed out.

For days the low lying areas of Lenoir and surrounding counties were flooding, wreaking havoc we hadn't previously seen.

*   *   *

So, I'm sitting here waiting for Isabel to approach. She's supposed to make landfall within the next hour or two in the vicinity of North Carolina's outer banks, about 70 miles east of us.

Being that far inland, we don't expect hurricane force winds to reach us. It was just announced the winds have already decreased from 150 mph to 100-even before hitting land. I expect this one to be a nuisance more than anything else. That means lots of water and winds just strong enough to fell a few trees. They are projected to reach 50 or 60 mph in our city. The storm's forward speed has just increased to 18 mph, according to a news bulletin. At that speed it should blow itself past our latitude before days end-and things should be calming down.

Since we are blessed (?) with lots of pine trees in our neighborhood, it's possible the area could lose one or two-but even that is doubtful.

When we purchased this lot it was completely covered with rows of pines, but we had all but fifteen removed before construction began. Over the years I've had fourteen of those removed. The only one left standing is in our front yard, as far away from the house as it can be.

Charlie, back of us, still has a mess of them and Carolyn-on our east side-still has a few. Some of them now appear to reach the stratosphere and are slowly becoming tall enough to be within striking distance of our dwelling, should one be toppled in our direction.

Our city is literally filled with pines, which some people value greatly-and consider them to be only a minor hazard which they choose to live with.

Betsey, on our west side, has eliminated the ones she inherited when she purchased the house a few years ago. No threat is posed from that direction.

I see Claude and Martha have moved their new car out of their pine filled yard and parked it in one stall of Carolyn's garage. They've also moved their other one into the open street, away from all trees. One can tell they have attended institutions of higher learning-in addition to having gone through a number of these things in the past.

Phone rings-"Ray, this is Carolyn; I'm over to Dan and Margaret's house." "Well, I see your car is still home-how did you get over there?" "Well, Dan came and got me (widows and orphans). Have you still got lights on Sutton Drive, Ray?" "Yes." "You have?" "Yeah, they flicked off and on a few times, but they're back on now." "Well, the ones over here at Dan's are out, but he has a generator." "That's what you get for leaving a neighborhood filled with great people and superior surroundings. I'm on the porch watching nature do her thing. If I notice a pine penetrating your roof, I'll give you a ring."

Ken, one block over, called about an hour ago and said they had lost their electrical current about noon. He was surprised to hear we still had ours. It probably won't be long before ours goes.

Anticipating that possibility, we decide to have our evening meal early in the afternoon, instead of at 5 p.m. At that time we can subsist on a can of Vienna sausage and crackers, should it come down to a no electrical power situation.

We are probably getting our strongest gusts about now. I notice some of the tallest and skimpiest trees are beginning to deviate about 45 degrees from their normal upright position. In one of these disturbances a few years ago I saw one of the pines snap about half way up and end up going through the roof of the house next door to Charlie, which is now occupied by Oscar.

I notice Michael's basketball goal is prostrate on our concrete drive. It's one of those heavy metal jobs that's anchored by a metal base filled with water. Uh, oh, there goes our power outage. It finally made its presence known.

The last news I heard on the tube before it became silent, was that landfall had been made on the NC coast with winds of about 80 mph.

It's now five o'clock-and despite some pretty strong gusts occasionally-the worst appears to be over.

Charlie called from Sparre Drive earlier to ask if we had current, saying his had been off for several hours. That means the outage must be fairly widespread. There must be a few trees leaning on power lines somewhere.

It has rained all day, but it hasn't come down like cats and dogs, as it does sometimes. Now the waiting game begins-we never know how long the outage will last. There are times when it can be restored within a few hours and at other times it takes days. We could have a long night coming up.

Our decision to cook our big meal at lunch turned out to be a good one. Now, in order to become nutritionally satisfied, we must partake of whatever we want to ingest prior to darkness-which we do.

I went to the supermarket yesterday and did all my pre-hurricane shopping. It consisted of purchasing three cans of Vienna sausage, a loaf of bread and three pears. We already possessed a jar of peanut butter. We were ready for bear.

Life is so full of choices-I can choose between sausage and nut butter-and I opt for the latter. I've always loved that stuff. Annie simply eats a pear-we both love fruit.

Darkness descends-no lights visible anywhere in the neighborhood-street lights all diminished. I earlier searched and found our two flashlights and made sure they were working-they were-and I procured a battery powered radio from the closet in Cindy's room and changed dead batteries for fresh ones. It used six "D's" and that's the exact number I found in the bedside table drawer. I now light a big candle and place it on a TV table-beside the two flashlights and radios and my spectacles. I really don't know why I'm concerned about the glasses.

Phone rings-I have to get up and find my way to the one mounted on the wall in the kitchen. The portable one became useless the instant we lost electric power-and we haven't chosen to join the cell phone race. I know that reverts us to the dark ages.

I finger the flash, turn it on and proceed to the phone. I know full well who will be on the other end and what Cindy's first five words will be. She doesn't disappoint me. "Daddy, what are you doing?" I give her my stock answer by replying, "Talking to you." I tell her what we have for light and she immediately comes forth with unsolicited advice. "Daddy, I've heard you're not supposed to burn candles if you have natural gas coming into your house." "Why?" "I don't know exactly-it has something to do with possible fumes and the flame on the candle." "Look, all we have is a water heater and it's closed up in the utility room. We've been using candles for years during hurricanes." "Well, I'm telling you what I heard." This is what we get for sending her to two state universities-a lot of unasked for advice.

Annie pops up and says she, too, had heard a little something on TV about the same subject. She feels a little edgy. My retort to her is, "At 80, asphyxiation might not be a bad way to go. Annie, would you feel better with that candle un-lit?" "Yes, I would." Deed done.

One of my next utterances: "Boy, I'll be glad when bedtime comes." There is little to be ecstatic about sitting with another person in a totally dark room waiting for bedtime to arrive. Being long time members of the geriatric generation, there isn't a whole lot to do. The only thing I can imagine more boring would be to sit totally alone. Every few minutes I click the flash to check the time by throwing the beam on the wall clock. My usual retiring time is 11:00. It occurs to me an individual has the prerogative to change his own bedtime if he so desires-and I suddenly decide to roll mine back to 10:00.

"Annie, I'm going to hit the sack and I'm leaving the brightest flash for you to find the bedroom when you decide to call it quits-and for getting to the john if need be."

I take the dimmer one because my room of relief is very close to my bed. In fact, if I should develop a yearning to go-and fall prostrate in the right direction-my torso would already be inside the W.C.

*   *   *

Five a.m. Friday, September 19-I'm up. Unfortunately, I was not awakened during the night by a suddenly blaring TV-nor a bright light-so I know our power is still off. Nevertheless, I'm ready to get things going, so I flash myself to the bathroom sink and give my body a quick cat bath in darkness. Since I know the location of all my body parts, it's no big deal. Shades of Normandy in World War II!

Annie is still asleep-something she knows how to do well. Its 5:45 and I get antsy, so I exit the porch door, stroll in the yard and am amazed at my surroundings. It's still dark-not one little sound to be heard. I don't believe even one pine needle is stirring-perfect stillness. Not a light to be seen anywhere. I look up at the sky and am overwhelmed by a most marvelous spectacle. Slightly east sits the most beautiful half-moon I've ever had the occasion to witness. It's extremely bright, without a blemish, and is attended by multitudes of heavenly bodies, including the big dipper, Mars and all the others. There isn't a wisp of a cloud in the entire sky-no fog-no pollution. It's as if God had used the waters of the hurricane to totally cleanse the universe. Surely, this is how God intended the heavens to look on a perfect night such as this.

I walk out to our paper-mailbox combo, knowing the Free Press can't be in its hole this early, especially after yesterday's storm, but it is. I also open the door of the mailbox, just for kicks, and there's a piece of mail in there. Where did it come from? Surely the USPS didn't deliver it yesterday in all that weather, but it must have. They can now add another word to their slogan: Rain, sleet, snow, dogs- and now hurricanes.

Six-forty, it's now light. I decide to ride around and see how things look. I refrain from opening the fridge for breakfast ingredients for fear of letting cold air escape. I need to check on breakfast possibilities, so I drive down to Vernon Avenue, aka "restaurant row". Some lights are on and a few businesses appear open. Bo jangles is closed and I can see why. The intersection just back of it is a mass of tangled wire-with a dangling transformer and a huge oak tree on top of it all. No telling when the city guys will get that mess unscrambled-enabling the popular fast food eatery to open its doors.

A few blocks east I can see McDonalds. It also has no lights- but across the street from it is Hardee's. It's open and business is thriving. "Give me two sausage biscuits to go." On my way home I notice numerous downed trees-mostly oaks-and I pass another dangling transformer on Herritage Street.

"Annie, get up, I've got food! Let's eat it before it gets cold. Just don't open the fridge-we'll drink water." This turns out to be a really good breakfast-biscuit brown and crisp-better than their biscuits used to be.

About 7:30 I decided to call the city emergency number to find out what's going on. "Sir, I know it's mighty early in the day, and I apologize for calling, but I need to know what plans to make today- and possibly for tonight. I see some people on lower Sutton Drive have lights on. Can you tell me if you think our power on the 1500 block will be on before nightfall?"

"Yes sir, I feel sure we'll get to you sometime today, but I don't know what time it will be." Good enough for me. Now I can confront the job ahead of me-cleaning up this yard that resembles the city dump. There's an accumulation of pine straw, pine cones, leaves, little branches and a few big ones.

By 3:00 I've finished cleaning the yard and even mowed the front grass, but there's still no power at Rouse's house. Annie says some ice cream would surely taste good but I still refuse to open the freezer compartment. I go to the supermarket and purchase a half gallon of all natural butter pecan, an apple and a banana.

We can't eat all the ice cream and we have nowhere to put what's left. "Carolyn-can you eat butter pecan ice cream?" "No, my stomach won't let me do it." "Betsey are you allowed to eat ice cream?" "No, Ray, my doctor won't let me." "Elizabeth, can you eat—-?" "Yes, bring me a serving."

In returning home I have to go through Charlie's yard, allowing me to run into him and ask the same question. "Thanks, but I have some in the freezer. By the way, I have a generator plugged into my freezer. Why don't you put the remainder of the carton in it? If you have anything else you would like to stick in it-feel free."

Now, that's what neighbors are for. At 4:00 Charlie sticks his head around the corner and hollers, "Power's on!" Great news! Annie immediately goes to the cereal cabinet-grabs a box and fills a bowl with the breakfast stuff and downs it with soy milk. She looks at me and says "Look at my hands-they're shaking. I hate hurricanes."

Postscript: Later records reveal that Isabel, at some point, was a category 5 storm while churning in the Atlantic-with winds reaching 165 mph. It covered an area about the size of Texas, creating havoc from South Carolina to Ontario, Canada.

When it made landfall in NC, winds had subsided to about 100 miles per hour. Fifty three people died as a result of the storm. Total damage amounted to over three billion dollars. Over four million people were without electrical power over the course of the blow.

Yes, Isabel wasn't much of a menace to Kinston, North Carolina, but to some areas she was no lady.

*   *   *

An occasional hurricane, be it weak or strong, is the price we pay for having close access to the sandy beaches of the Atlantic Ocean. But that's offset by their beauty in times of calmness. Not only are the waters of the deep magnificent, there are other beautiful scenes to view.

Case in point:

See-Sea

When I strolled down
To see the sea,
It was the sea
I meant to see.

When I arrived there
'Twas apparent to me,
There was much more
Than sea to see.

First seen were Sapiens-
Great hordes of them.
Some big and round,
Others thin, I found.

I spied one fem
With figure so grand.
In a suit so scant
Why wasn't it banned?

A string at the bottom,
Another at the top.

I wondered if maybe
The top might pop.

So did some guys
Following close behind.
Willing to assist her
Should she get in a bind.

Then other beauts followed
One after the other,
With their own entourage
And not enough cover.

'Twas enough to make
An old man stutter
And make him wonder
Can it get any better?

The last Queen passed
And I asked myself:
What had I come
To the sea to see?

Let's go back to the cartoon a few chapters back depicting the motorist in the middle of nowhere waiting for the traffic light to change. When I first noted the thing I began guessing as to the locale of the event. First of all, it just about had to be west of the Mississippi, that old man river that just keeps rolling along.

It also had to be in an area of great vastness, flat enough for persons to see for miles-and as straight as an arrow. It could have been set in any number of Southwestern states, but I placed it in the southern state of Texas. In 1951, Annie and I traveled over a number of roads in that huge state that would have qualified as the setting.

We passed through one area in which the roads were so straight and minus of traffic that I even allowed Annie to drive. That took courage. When we married in 1947 she was not a driver. I attempted to instruct her in the art of driving a straight shift vehicle-without success. I finally turned the job over to a driving instructor and paid him to put his life on the line. I don't know what his charge was, but it was worth it. She succeeded in obtaining a driver's license and, at this point, she's never had an at fault accident-no traffic violations.

I recall spotting another cartoon in a newspaper eons ago in which there was no question of the locale. It pictured a man sitting on a toilet seat, with this caption inscribed at the bottom of the cartoon: "The only man in Washington who knows what he's doing." My feeling is-if he's still there-bring him out. We need him badly to solve a few hundred problems. We truly need problem solvers and I don't personally see any waiting in the wings.

I've been thinking of a group that might be able to help us out, a group you would probably never consider. Psychiatrists! Yes-shrinks!

Think about it-they face new problems every week. When M.D.'s see a patient for the first time, that person usually has an ailment that the doctor has been confronted with previously.

Psychiatrists, on the other hand, are often asked to solve problems, the nature of which they are not familiar. In such cases they oftentimes have to come up with off the wall suggested cures.

Take the case of Louise and George. They had been married about ten years and had gotten along fairly amicably, but George had a "collection" problem. He loved newspapers and magazines and had been storing them around the house since shortly after their wedding. He had copies of "Playboy", "Peanuts", and other periodicals going back for years. He first stashed them in the attic until it was full. Then he had to go to the family's living space. After utilizing all closet space, he then began piling them under their beds. We all know how many things can be stored under our beds. They are great places to slide three or four pairs of shoes, even boxes stored with off season clothes. Even a few pieces of exercise paraphernalia can be crammed under them.

Louise had been after George for several years to rid the house of those paper products for which they had no need. She got nowhere. She was at wits end and finally, without George knowing it, she saw a psychiatrist. She explained the family's problem to him and asked for his advice. Doc put his grey matter to work and finally said, "Louise, why don't you simply go home and announce to George that you are going to ask for a divorce unless he gets rid of every old newspaper and magazine there is in the house-and put a time limit on it."

This was a rather drastic, suggested remedy to her problem, but she was tired of stumbling over piles of papers and magazines and was willing to try anything. She decided to put her foot down.

After dinner that night she sat down with George and broke the news to him. "George, either the papers go, or I go. Two weeks!"

She could hardly have been more outspoken. The ball was in George's court. Let's see what he did with it.

He certainly was not surprised. He had seen this coming for sometime. He had a choice to make-did he want to keep the papers-or Louise? He knew he couldn't have both. He really had a strong attachment to those papers, but they could not cook, iron, wash dishes, look after kids, nor be a good bedfellow.

He would force himself to get rid of the papers-but how? There were, of course, many ways to do away with papers. He could sell, or even give them to a fish market to be used as wrappers. He could burn them, throw them away as trash for the city to pick up, or donate them to a family in the country who might still be using a two-holer.

We all have heard the expression, "You can't have your cake and eat it too." Was there some way he could get rid of those papers and yet, somehow, keep them?

While sitting on their back steps pondering his predicament, his eyes fell on a fairly large hole in the middle of the yard. It had been created recently when a hurricane blew over a small tree. He had disposed of the tree but had not filled the hole. Solution! He would bury those papers in that hole. He had promised Louise he would come up with a way to eliminate the papers within two weeks-and he had.

The deed would be done. But just how would this best be accomplished? After all, there were good neighbors on each side of them and he didn't especially want to tell the neighborhood exactly what he was doing. If Sam should come out his back door, see him and ask what he was doing-what could he tell him? Maybe Sue would see him and holler, "What are you doing George, digging your grave?"

One possibility would be to bury those rascals at night, when nobody would see him. That might work unless Sam should come home after a night on the town and see him dumping bundles of "something" into a hole, resulting in a call being made to the local cop station-reporting him on suspicion of laying out a "Pet Sematary".

After filling his mind with as much mental engrossment as he thought it could withstand, he made a decision. He would simply walk out back-dig the hole to make it deeper-and fill it with the product. If either neighbor should come out and ask the obvious, he would simply reply, "I'm filling this hole with newspapers-are you blind?"

He did it. He got a shovel from the storage room and strolled in broad daylight to the backyard. He made advancement to the cavity and enlarged it sufficiently to contain his problem.

He never had looked upon a shovel with affection-and this particular job did nothing to improve upon that feeling-but he completed the task. After giving his back a short time to recover, he began the ritual of going into the house, grabbing armfuls of papers and carrying them to the hole. There were lots of papers and lots of trips through the house and he never stumbled once. He cleaned the house of every paper in sight and he still had room at the top of the hole to fill it with several inches of soil. Job well done. Mission accomplished. He got rid of the papers as promised. The shrink had solved the problem.

Psychiatrists, as one would imagine, are butts of many jokes. There was one making the rounds a year or so ago that caught my attention-which I consider worthy of being passed along.

There were pre-teen twin boys who were just about identical in appearance. They also had many of the same traits; however, in one aspect they were one hundred percent adverse. Sam was an eternal optimist-no matter how dark a situation appeared to be-no matter what obstacles were thrown in his path, he was convinced things would turn out favorably in the end.

Jamie, on the other hand, looked on every event from a pessimistic viewpoint. He always regarded the future as dismal and he expected the worst to result from any problem encountered.

Their mother was concerned over Jamie's attitude and decided to consult a psychiatrist to seek a possible solution to his terrible attitude. The mother presented the facts to the doctor during the initial session, which was about two weeks before Christmas. Being asked for suggested solutions, the doctor came up with one.

"Mrs. Smith, your predicament is a challenging one, but I have a suggestion that might lead to some kind of solution. This Christmas, I want you to give Jamie the nicest gifts you can find. If you know his favorite colors I want you to include them-just do everything you can to please him. As for Sam, I want you to give him nothing but a simple box of manure." No questions asked by mother. Suggestion complied with.

Christmas morn-gift opening time. Mom cracked the door to Jamie's room to take a peek at his reaction to the wonderful gifts she had so carefully chosen for him. There he was-throwing a tantrum and muttering to himself. The toys were made by the wrong manufacturer. He hated the colors, the clothing items were not his style. Nothing was right.

She closed the door and went to Sam's room, cracked the door, and saw him reaching both hands in the open box of manure and joyfully throwing it into the air.

"Sam, what in the world are you doing?" "Mom, with all this stuff, there's just got to be a pony here somewhere!"

Why Izzits and Remember Whens

Why izzit-we get red blood from blue blood vessels?

Why izzit-when we're in our thirties and forties, when we really need more home space, we can't afford it-and when in our sixties and seventies and can afford it-we don't need it?

Why izzit-we have to endure 1 hour of TV commercials in order to view a two hour movie? It has gotten to the point that with so many commercial breaks, one can get a better understanding of the plot by reading a simple preview of the movie. I have become so disgusted with movie breaks on network TV, that I've been watching commercial-free movies recently on TCM. I'd rather watch an old movie in one piece than a recent release that's chopped up in hundreds of pieces.

Of course, I could be in a class by myself. I read recently that lots of schools are now allowing Channel One, whose parent company is PRIMEDIA, to show news stories to students. By allowing this program into the schools, the students become captive audiences for the commercials being shown by advertisers. Recent studies have shown that students remember more of the advertising than they do the news stories.

As much as I dislike commercials, I must admit there are some which seem to have a lasting impression on me. You know, our country-or maybe the world-seems to be caught up in fears of contamination. The first thing we look for in a restaurant is the poster on a wall showing the latest sanitary rating. When we enter a fast food establishment and notice the food handlers preparing the items barehanded, we want to holler out, "Hey bud, why don't you put on gloves?" And how about public restrooms? When we leave home, we can only hope we don't have an "urge" before returning home.

An ad that impressed me recently depicts a handsome businessman who has just turned his financial portfolio over to an attractive female investment advisor for handling. He is on his way to treat her for lunch-revealing to her audibly that he has great faith in her ability to enhance the value of his assets. The fact she was a real "looker" had not influenced him in any way, I'm sure.

As they reach the elevator, she reaches over to punch "down". He grabs her arm, pushes the button himself, and admonishes her, "Germs, you know." There is one other male passenger in the cage. When the vehicle reaches ground level and the door opens, the passenger coughs. When this catastrophic event occurs the investor gently wraps his arm around the waist of his female companion and rushes her out. At the same time, he turns his head and glowers at that poor innocent guy and says, "Why don't you take that sick day, pal?" Strange thing-I don't remember the sponsor.

And that, somehow, reminds me of a unique license plate I saw recently on back of a retired school teachers car. It read, "I used up all my sick days, so I called in dead."

I'll admit-even I see an ad occasionally that's more entertaining than the program, itself. I saw two recently that could fall in this category.

The first one opened with three or four smaller kids leaning on a chain link fence-looking into the yard next door. They were eyeing their Frisbee which was lying beside the neighbor's doghouse right in the middle of the neighbor's yard. Nabor had a dog, a yapping one which was letting the kids know they were not welcome in his territory, Frisbee or no Frisbee. Don't know what the dog's name was-could have been "Mighty Mite." He (or she) was on a leash that was tied to the doghouse-and its length reached to within about two feet of the fence.

Here comes an older kid on a bike and he notes the consternation on the faces of the younger ones. He wants to help them out. He thinks for just a moment and scrambles over the fence. "Mite" sees him immediately and makes a direct dash toward him, as if he were a rabbit to be devoured. About one foot away from the youngster, the leash ran out. The kid was safe from the fangs of the little, but ferocious sounding animal. Timmy had formulated a plan when he jumped that fence and now was the time to put it in action. It was time to see which would prevail-man or beast!

Timmy began slowly moving counter clockwise in a circle around the doghouse, staying just out of the reach of the dog. With each circle the leash wrapped around the doghouse, making it shorter each time. Shortly, when there were only a couple of feet left, Timmy dashed for the Frisbee and ran to the fence, scaling it before Mite could unwind the leash. Another victory for man over beast.

Another one-same sponsor. This little girl kid appeared to be about three or four years old and might have been in an office building with her dad. It seems that her dad had made her one of those paper airplanes that we used to make and sail it cross a room-sometimes a classroom before the teacher arrived. When Jane launched it the thing didn't land on the floor, as anticipated. It settled down atop a cabinet about five feet tall. Consternation! She didn't want to bother her dad, who was working in the room next door. In the wink of an eye she opened a drawer at the bottom of the cabinet and pulled out a stack of computer paper, hauled it across the floor and placed it on the floor directly below a window location. The window was one of those jobs with three narrow oblong panes that will open when you pull a lever down.

Jane steps on the stack of paper that puts her just high enough to reach the lever with her fingertips. She pulls on the lever and all three panes open wide, allowing a breeze from outside to rush in and blow her beloved plane off the cabinet onto the floor. There's more than one way to skin a cat. What ingenuity these kids have nowadays!

And how about those large newspaper ads, which usually promote expensive items. In big print they tell us of the attributes of the product, but at the very bottom of the ad there's very fine print that isn't readable to the naked eye. A few days ago I saw one that mirrored the one just described. I procured my magnifying glass from a den shelf, but to no avail. Is there something in that fine print they don't want us to know about?

Why izzit-the cost of the present Iraq and Afghanistan wars are not included in our federal budget as a regular expenditure? The president's economic advisor in 2002 predicted the wars might ultimately cost us up to two-hundred billion dollars. A newspaper item I saw just a few days ago stated that the wars so far have cost us $440 billion and the cost is still climbing. Present costs are in excess of $5 billion per month and none of this is showing up in the budget. Do we need to wonder at what point in time our country simply implodes?

Why izzit-when stock prices decline the so called pros on Wall Street can blame it on a poor economy-unemployment rate is too high. The next month the market declines again in spite of a good employment report. This time they say the decline is due to too many people working-which denotes future inflation. Those guys are smart?

Why izzit-restaurant employees pack table napkins so tight in their containers that you need pliers to extract them?

Why izzit-every presidential candidate-when running for office-says he's for smaller government; but before the oval office chair cushion gets warm, the boss begins making the institution larger? Same old political gobbledygook!

*   *   *

Remember when-Coca Cola had a lock on the cola drink industry, and along comes Pepsi-Cola-born in New Bern, in our state of North Carolina? Suddenly, instead of paying a nickel for a 6 ounce Coke, we could get 12 ounces of Pepsi for the same 5 cent piece. When I was a kid we could get a Pepsi, plus a package of sweet rolls for a dime. When that five cent sweet roll was first introduced, it was covered with white icing and I thought it was lard-until I bit into it and tasted that sweet morsel. That five cent package contained four rolls and I could eat the whole package at a time. I saw a package similar to the original in a local supermarket, price-$1.79.

Remember when-you had to go to a prison in order to see a window with metal bars? Now just go around the corner in many neighborhoods.

Remember when-we could stand up on two legs and put both feet in trousers without falling down or grabbing a bed post?

I have a friend who recently put one foot up on a chair to tie her shoe strings. She lost her balance and fell to the floor, breaking a hip. There seems to be danger just about everywhere for the geriatric generation in which a lot of us live.

Remember when-we could buy a Baby Ruth, Milky Way, Butterfinger, and others for one cent?

I can remember my brother buying an old 1924 Chrysler Convertible. He paid $12.50 for it and the seller let him pay it off at the rate of 50 cents per week. His wages for working in tobacco fields that summer amounted to 35 cents per day-not per hour.

Remember when-they (whomever "they" were) advised us to invest in America by buying common stock? Don't hear that anymore. When you purchase shares now, you are buying chances on a roulette wheel.

Remember when-traveling show people would set up a tent in the neighborhood and put on a show for the purpose of hawking snake oil as a cure-all for almost any ailment?

I heard a person recently tell about an experience she had years ago in a sideshow. The huckster was telling his audience how wonderful his product was. He claimed that, if taken as prescribed, it would actually take years off a person's age. To make his point, he asked a lady from the audience to take a bottle and go behind a curtain, follow directions on the bottle, and come back to the audience in 15 minutes-so they could see just how much younger she would look.

The crowd waited expectantly and when time had expired the forty-five year old lady who had gone back of the curtain came out in the person of an 18 year old girl! The audience went wild with laughter and still bought the snake oil!

I saw an ad in a trade magazine the other week that really boosted a new type tomato plant. One plant would produce sixty pounds of tomatoes-the fruit weighing up to two pounds each. A grower would have the equivalent of a tomato farm with just one plant that would grow 8 feet tall in just two months and would produce tomatoes from summer to fall. The plants were currently on sale at two for $6.98. Question: why would you need TWO?

Travel

Back in the days of yore, when television was really entertaining and filth hadn't yet been factored into it, I enjoyed such shows as "All in the Family", "The Lawrence Welk Show", "Bonanza", and "The Honeymooners", among some others. I especially liked the latter one in which Jackie Gleason always said, "Give me a little traveling music."

Someone over the years should have coined the phrase, "A little traveling is good for the soul." We were fortunate enough to take several extended trips, and I was never more at ease than when on a trip. It was nice to leave worries behind for a while.

When authoring "They Didn't Bring Ice" I highlighted a number of those trips, but there was one I left out. This one occurred in summer of 1982. We were accompanied by Annie's sister, Eleanor, and her husband, Louis-who were subjects of an earlier chapter in this book.

Before leaving Kinston I took the Pontiac Lemans to the dealer with instructions to check it over in order to determine if any repairs were needed. I had never done that prior to any other journey we had undertaken. No problems were found. They even gave us a free wash job, which meant the car was looking good when we picked up the Smiths in Goldsboro.

We headed west, then north. Before driving too many miles-and having reached West Virginia-I heard a scraping noise from underneath the car. After hearing it scrape for a while, I pulled onto the shoulder and stopped. Louis got out, kneeled down and recognized the problem. He immediately took care of it, but when we drove off we were missing one body part-a muffler. Louis had kicked it off and thrown it into a roadside ditch. Why hadn't the guys at the garage seen the rusted out device and replaced it? So much for having a car inspected prior to a trip. I never did it again. Not even when preparing for a seven week trip later in life.

It was Saturday afternoon-bad time to catch auto repair shops open. The first town we reached, still in West Virginia, was Charleston,

I believe. I looked for a Sears and found one with a body shop that was open. We left the shop with a less noisome vehicle than when we entered it. We were lucky. Next stop was Dayton, Ohio, where we spent the night.

We departed early Sunday morning and headed for Niagara Falls. Annie and I had visited there previously, but the Smiths never had, and they made the most of it-including taking a boat ride to the base of the falls on the "Maid of the Mist".

After leaving the Canadian side of the falls, we remained in the area and toured the School of Horticulture floral gardens, which exhibited a wonderful array of flowers. The girls had their picture taken standing in front of the floral clock.

Driving north we passed through the small town of St. Catherine, and it was there that we bought the most delicious peaches from a roadside stand that I have ever tasted. We then entered the city of Toronto, one of Canada's major cities. We tarried there just long enough to inspect the CN tower, which had become a Canadian landmark. We drove around the entire north side of Lake Ontario to the city of Cornwall, where we crossed the beautiful St. Lawrence River to again enter the US. We stopped in Vermont long enough for Eleanor to wet her feet in Lake Champlain and pick up a few shells.

In Portland, Maine, we stopped to visit my nephew, Ernest Malloy and his wife Joan. They were expecting us and Joan had a nice spread of hors d'oeuvres to whet our appetite. Afterward,

Ernest called several seafood restaurants to check out lobster prices-
and he found one serving doubles for $7.50. We had a nice meal and
an enjoyable visit with a nephew who had spent a good portion of
his youthful life with our family in North Carolina.

Adjacent to Portland is Cape Elizabeth, which is home to one
of the most famous lighthouses in our country and is situated on
the shores of the Atlantic Ocean. It is one of four colonial lighthouses authorized by George Washington and dedicated by General
Lafayette. In 1788, congress appropriated money and engaged
two stone masons from Portland to work on the structure that was
completed in 1790. It was first lighted January 10, 1791, with the
use of whale oil lamps-later changed to kerosene. Today the light is
an airport type beacon with 1,000 watt lamp lens of 200,000 candle
power and is visible for approximately twenty miles.

Upon leaving Maine, we resumed our southern course and found
ourselves in Salem, Massachusetts. Having read of the place years
back in public school history books, we took the opportunity to
research our memory of events that had taken place there. In addition
to being site of the infamous witch trials of 1692, it was home of the
House of Seven Gables, the structure that inspired author Nathaniel
Hawthorne to write his legendary novel of the same name. Being the
oldest surviving 17th century wooden mansion in New England, the
structure was given a good going over before leaving the city.

As for witch trials, they had occurred during an era in which
there was strong belief in the devil and witchcraft in the area of

Salem. That being the case, it was no surprise when two young sick girls who failed to respond to generally accepted medical treatment, accused certain residents of afflicting them by witchcraft. They claimed it had caused them incurable pain. The accused were found guilty in a court of law and death sentences were pronounced upon them. Within a three day period a total of nineteen men and women were hanged for supposedly engaging in the crime of witchcraft.

Next stop: Hyannis Port-a few miles south of Salem and home of the "Kennedy Compound". The exclusive Kennedy clan residences could only be seen from offshore in Nantucket Sound. Inside the town only the rooftops were visible. The family seemed to be blocked off from townspeople.

A few miles south of Hyannis Port lies the small village of Woods Hole, from which several ferries departed daily to Martha's Vineyard. It was just a few miles offshore-not nearly as far as Nantucket Island is from Hyannis Port. Inasmuch as weather was great and a ferry was taking on passengers, we decided to take the boat trip.

The bay at the island was filled with moored sailboats, as the bay at Woods Hole had been. It was not difficult to ascertain that the place was not a hangout for the underprivileged. Once on the island we decided to take a bus tour of the place, which didn't take long. The island is only about twenty-five miles long with a maximum width of about seven miles. Having a modest year-round population of about 15,000-it is said to swell during summer months to about one hundred thousand.

The island's coastline was adorned by clay bluffs, which somehow reminded one of the White Clifes of Dover, only on a much smaller scale, and having a different hue. We discovered that the island was also the possessor of a lighthouse, albeit not as renowned as the one at Cape Elizabeth.

During World War II the island was the beneficiary of a shot in the arm from America's military establishment. An air base was constructed there at which airmen learned gunnery, and also how to take off and land on aircraft carriers. The island's beach area had also been used for practicing beach landings preparatory to the real thing on France's Normandy beaches on June 6, 1944.

After the war, the island had been transformed into a playground for the rich and famous, with a number of celebrities establishing summer homes there. At the time of our visit, Jackie Kennedy had a home there, but our bus tour did not include a trip by it. The tour guide mentioned that he occasionally met her on the road while doing tours.

Adjacent to the island was a much smaller one named Chappaquiddick, which is connected to the Vineyard by a wooden bridge. It was on that bridge that an accident had taken place that made national headlines. On July 19, 1969, Senator Edward Kennedy drove his auto off the wooden bridge, drowning a young female democrat campaign worker by the name of Mary Jo Kopechne. He fled the scene of the accident, waiting several hours before reporting it to the police.

Not only did he escape serious injury in the accident, he was also able to avoid legal penalties-and didn't even suffer in the polls at the next election. The Kennedy name carried a lot of weight in Massachusetts-and it still does.

A tragic accident involving another Kennedy would take place in the same vicinity in 1999. John Kennedy, Jr., the senator's nephew, would be killed in a plane crash just off Martha's Vineyard's shore, along with his wife and her sister.

When we debarked at Woods Hole we asked about restaurants and were informed there was a very well known one right beside the water and we trekked to it.

When we were seated we were advised by the very young waitress that the chef's specialty was a fruit plate at the price of $7.50. Annie ordered it and we other three ordered something less ornate. The waitress was correct; the plate of fruit was beautiful and was consumed without difficulty by Mrs. Rouse. The waitress also informed us we were dining in a very famous geodesic eatery. I asked her what the word geodesic meant. Her answer: "I don't know."

We had one more stop to make before heading home. It was to attend the wedding of a niece, daughter of my brother Woodrow. They had also lived with us periodically in their early years. Now, Rosemary Rouse was about to join hands with Ken Schulze to become man and wife in the yard of a beautiful old white frame home, with adjoining carriage house, in New York state. Isn't it strange how I managed to see a nephew and a niece, neither of whom I had seen for ages, in the same trip without altering our route?

When we received our invitation to the wedding I considered it just a formality. We certainly would not be able to attend. Then I double checked our itinerary and discovered that it called for us to be traveling very close to the wedding site on the exact date of the wedding!

It was a beautiful day and the wedding was the same. The yard was attractively decorated-with a number of musicians in place ready to do their thing. The ceremony was carried out without a hitch. Tables were set up under a tent and were loaded with delicacies. Unfortunately, we were unable to remain and participate in their consumption. We were a little behind in our schedule and needed to move on.

Good-byes were said and we headed south-straight through New York City on I-95. Nice trip.

Gas

How can I cover "life" without discussing that commodity we call gasoline, that absolutely essential ingredient that was instrumental in taking us to Ontario and getting us back to North Carolina?

I feel somewhat qualified to talk about it because I worked around it a little, many years ago.

My brother, Biggie, operated a service station. Some Saturdays I worked for him since my permanent job was a five day sort of thing.

Those times were prior to the self service era. Every customer had to be waited on personally. My job was mainly pumping gas, but that was not all that was required in the process. We were expected to check the oil, check the water, check the battery and wash the windshield. We were even asked to check air in tires and look at fan belts. All this was expected regardless of the amount of gas purchased-which was most often five gallons. The price was in the neighborhood of thirty cents per gallon. That was less than the amount of tax we have to pay now on each gallon, which runs about fifty three cents in North Carolina.

Due to those circumstances, it was always nice to hear a customer say "Fill it up".

In those days there never was a shortage of gas. The shortage occurred in the financial ability to pay for it. The first shortage in the product that I can recall occurred in World War II and, since I wasn't a civilian, it didn't bother me. We seemed to have sufficient supply of it in my military unit.

The first shortage of the product I was involved in came about years after the war ended. It must have been about 3 decades, or more, ago. It seems that OPEC got riled up over something and decided to cut the supply of the precious stuff. It was very difficult to find a service station that had a supply of gas. When we found one word would spread and motorists would descend on it.

Station operators would limit the number of gallons a customer could purchase. The amount would sometimes be as little as 5 gallons. When supply was cut off we would shake the nozzle to be sure we got every drop we had paid for. They rarely instructed us to "fill it up". After a lot of weeks normal supplies were restored, but one thing had been proven: We were at the mercy of the oil industry and it could use the big stick as it desired.

Our present situation is diverse. There is plenty of gasoline out there, but at great cost, which at times has exceeded three dollars per gallon. At time of this writing it is priced at $2.52. What it will be tomorrow is anybody's guess. At these prices, one would assume we would cut down our driving and conserve, but that doesn't appear to be the case. America is not a nation of conservatives, so we take other measures to lessen the pain. One is rather unique that I ran across some weeks ago. I was pumping petrol into my tank at a local station and a young girl drove up in an SUV. One of those big jobs that looks about as long as a box car. As she took the spout off the hook I made a comment concerning the high cost of the fuel. She astounded me by saying, "Oh, I don't let it bother me; I just buy ten dollars worth at the time anyway.???"

In a way, I've adopted a somewhat similar attitude. I've always automatically filled it up when pumping the fuel but when extremely high prices hit us, I became belligerent. I have a mid-size car and

$20 would fill the tank, previously, so I decided I wouldn't put in more than $25 worth at the time-just to get back at the oil companies. I later changed that maximum to $30, a limit at which I still stand. I don't "fill it up".

I still like that phrase, though, those three words, "fill it up", have a nice ring-and we still use it in a number of situations.

While in training camps during World War II, breakfast menus were usually pretty good. They consisted of fresh scrambled eggs, sausage, bacon, french toast, grits, and other stuff; however, it was a whole new ball game when we left the States. As a rule we lived on canned rations, but once in a while it became convenient for the portable kitchen to come up and serve a hot meal. When that happened, the favored breakfast item became creamed beef, better known to G.I.'s as S.O.S. I didn't like that stuff, so I didn't eat it if anything else was available. Now, when they had pancakes that was right up my alley. When I passed my mess kit in front of that delectable item and they asked "how many", my answer was always the same. "Fill it up".

Another favorite occasion at which to use this phrase is while dining out-when the waitress points to your cup and asks, "Coffee, sir?" you probably answer, "Fill it up".

On one such occasion at Ballantine's in Raleigh, NC, the three word phrase had a backfire effect, so to speak. After the meal had arrived and I had drunk about a half cup of the beverage, the waitress walked quietly by. She saw my half-empty cup and filled it to the brim with hot-very hot-java without uttering a word. I was busy eating and talking to Annie and had paid no attention to actions of the waitress. After finishing a heavy bite of delicious breaded veal cutlet, I automatically took cup in hand and took a big gulp to drown the cutlet. What do you think you would have done-sitting there in a public place with dozens of patrons all around you? How would you have prevented a spectacle, while holding a mouthful of coffee which was obviously 212°Fahrenheit?

It was definitely too hot to swallow and I certainly didn't want to spray it all over the area. Especially not on Annie and the kids, who would have probably suffered third degree burns.

I began swishing it around my mouth with great velocity, hoping my mouth flesh would cool it before it cracked my molars. During the time I was swishing, I was also turning my head side to side, thinking that might also help. Annie looked at me as if to ask, "What in the world are you doing?" The tactic worked. I finished my meal, suffering from nothing worse than a burned tongue. Off we trod to see "The Sound of Music".

Even though our present gas situation seems dire, there might be light at the end of the tunnel. Someone once made the remark that there's something good in every circumstance. Maybe some good will eventually come out of our present predicament. Maybe it will wake up our powers-to-be to the fact we need to discover something that can be used to power our vehicles, heat our homes, and run our machinery-and make us less dependent on oil.

There are some signs of this happening at the present. Already we are having some cars come off the assembly line that are hybrid-using battery power to supplement gasoline power. There also is limited use of ethanol-derived from corn-to power vehicles. Now they are talking about getting the substance from such things as other grains and grass.

There was a newspaper article I read the other day, and I'm sure a lot of you did, about a potentially new source of energy. Pet poop-can you believe that? Think about it-poop power! If pets, why not other animals? And I'm thinking big, really BIG-elephants! Think of the potential there.

When I was a kid, Kinston's slogan was, "Worlds foremost tobacco center". At one time one of our radio stations used "WFTC" as its call letters. Tobacco was big here and it was necessary to have lots of big trucks to haul it away from the auction warehouses to storage facilities. There were usually several bundles that fell off the trucks en route-and we would pick them up and re-sell them for a nickel a bundle.

That prompts me to visualize a bunch of elephants in a circus parade. Just imagine how much refuse they might eject onto the pavement in a two mile parade. One might follow them with a pail and scoop and come up with a small fortune. Not only that, the streets would become cleaner.

We are told that the beautiful and immaculately clean city of San Francisco is exploring the possibility of finding ways to turn the city's animal feces, which make up 4 percent of the city's residential waste, into methane that could be piped into anything powered by natural gas. If successful, the city could post a "Feces Free City" sign at the city limits.

I feel better about our gasoline conundrum already.

———————

Well, it looks like the long-standing debate between the believers of evolution versus believers of creationism will never die. I read recently in a newspaper article that evolution was being taught in a school in some state, but the creation theory was not. This seemed to be causing some consternation among the creation crowd.

Teachers on both sides are extremely sincere in their beliefs-and sometimes use bizarre analogies to impress the children.

Case in point: It was a cool day in April in a school in New England. It was the day before a two day school holiday. Miss Jones, who was explaining the theory of evolution to her class of seven year olds, wanted to make an impression strong enough to be retained by the children for several days.

She said: "Tommy, I want you to leave your seat and go over to the window. Now, Tommy, do you see the earth out there?" "Yes ma'am." "Tommy, do you see that big oak tree growing out of the earth?" "Yes ma'am." "Now, Tommy, I want you to look upward. Do you see that beautiful blue sky up there?" "Yes, Miss Jones, I see the sky." "Tell me Tommy, do you see God up there?" "No ma'am, I don't."

"That's the point I want you to take home with you today. Tommy did not see God because there was no God to see. Tommy didn't see God because God does not exist!"

Immediately, a seven year old girl sitting on the back row raised her hand. She was a smart little kid and didn't take everything for gospel. "Miss Jones, may I ask Tommy some questions?" "Yes, Mary, you may do so."

"Tommy, do you see Miss Jones standing up there?" "Yes, Mary, I do." "Do you see her arms and legs?" "Yes." "Do you see her neck?" "I do." "Tell me Tommy, do you see her brain?" "No, I don't see her brain." "Well, if we believe what she taught us today, she doesn't have one."

Someone once asked me if I had ever seen a miracle. My answer was in the negative. He then said, "Go home and look in a mirror."

It "Ain't" Like It Used To Be

A few weeks back I read an article that substantiated something I have known for quite some time. The headline stated that music is too expensive and is not very good. Three out of every four music fans polled complained that compact discs are too expensive. Actually, I can't personally contradict nor verify that opinion. The few we have were gifts. I can, however, agree with the second portion of the article: music nowadays is not very good. Maybe I was simply spoiled by the music of the big band era-the 1940 period. That was great music to dance by, smooch by and just listen to. Even go to sleep with. You can't do that now, unless you're still watching the Lawrence Welk Show on PBS. In fact, music now won't let you go to sleep, even if you have a notion to do so.

Music just isn't what it used to be. It's not just us oldies who feel this way. A poll showed that half the fans age 18-34 say music is getting worse. Could this be due to advent of the boom box? A few months ago I was a member of a church congregation that was exposed to artificial music and the "box" was turned up so loud I couldn't tell whether the guy was singing or a train was passing by.

And who are all these new guitar pickers I've seen on country music channels recently? It seems like when I'm away from that stuff for a few months and come back to it, there's a whole new covey whom I don't recognize. Before the program is over, it's made known that one of them has just made a record that sold over a million copies.

Whatever happened to musicians like Guy Lombardo, Harry James, Tommy Dorsey, and Glenn Miller? And vocalists like Bing Crosby, Nat King Cole, Judy Garland, and Peggy Lee? When they left the scene due to death or retirement, it seems they were not really replaced. Will that smooth voice of Perry Como ever be equaled?

Music is not the only thing that has deteriorated in recent years. Have you looked at roofing shingles on housetops in your neighborhood lately? On many of them it's difficult to determine what their original color was. Now they all appear to be black a few years after installment. They tell me it's fungus that causes them to turn black. Shingles I had installed on the first two houses we built retained their color until the warranty expired. And many other products are inferior to their predecessors.

Just a few years ago we replaced entrance doors of our church and planned to install new lock assemblies along with the doors. When we had a locksmith look at the old locks, his comments went something like this: "There is nothing available now that's as good as the old locks. Do yourself a favor and put the old ones back on."

The same thing appears to apply to wall-to-wall carpet: We are presently in the process of replacing carpet in three rooms that has been there for thirty years. Except for normal wear it still looks good. It still holds its original shape-no sign of stretching.

We put new carpet in our family room about ten years ago and it has stretched all over the place. We are now replacing it. I recently cut out a piece of the older carpet and looked at the backing. It was constructed of very fine mesh. I am told, by old carpet people, that was the reason it hadn't stretched. In shopping for carpet I kept looking at the back of samples for just such a mesh, but I found none.

I was told by salespeople: "They don't make that kind anymore." Where is all that technology we hear so much about?

Do you remember-when carpet was sold by the square yard? I wonder how much the cost to the consumer probably increased when the unit was changed from the square yard to square foot. Look out-I understand they are going to metric soon.

And how about those used-to-be one half gallons of ice cream cartons? They are now eight ounces lighter. Was the price reduced? Not hardly. That's what you call good marketing.

Have you noticed that financial institutions, in their newspaper ads, indicate the interest rates as being on an annual percentage YIELD instead of annual percentage RATE?

Dreams

"Dream when you're feeling blue. Dream-that's the thing to do. Dream when the smoke rings climb through the air, you'll find your share of happiness there."

Those were some of the approximate words to an old song back yonder when music was a joy to listen to.

"Good night-sweet dreams"-remember when you spoke those words to your three year old when you kissed her and pulled the covers up?

"I'll see you in my dreams." I believe that was the finishing line to the song shown above.

"I'll keep you in my dreams." Words a soldier tells his girlfriend as he kisses her and boards ship headed for a combat zone.

Dreams-a part of most peoples' lives. Some are sweet-some are not. I believe most of them are screwy. Some are frightening.

For a number of years after my military discharge I had a recurring dream about the war. It always involved the same thing. I was on a housetop and was being shot at by the pilot of a German fighter plane. I was hiding behind the brick chimney to avoid being hit by the bullets. The dream never lasted long enough for me to know how it came out. The last thing I saw each night was myself being crouched behind the chimney and the plane was coming straight for me. Within a period of two or three years the dream ceased. I've never had it since.

Some dreams do involve nice happenings and fall in the "sweet" category. Others, however, fall in a totally different one. Dreams become nightmares for some-who wish to heavens they could wake up and cut them off. Take Annie, for instance, she has some doozies. Let me relate a few to you.

"Almost every night I dream of wanting to pick up some object, but can't lift it, even though it's small and lightweight. I always get frustrated."

"I was in the back seat of a car with mama and daddy, and I said I wanted to get out of it. Mama turned around-looking terrible with snaggle-tooth teeth. She looked at me and said, 'A little boy has been abused and your husband did it!' 'That's not true; Ray wouldn't do a thing like that.' I told her to stop-I wanted to get out of the car."

"I was at college in my room and Jane was with me. She was a small child and she had a little dog with her. I was afraid school authorities might hear the dog bark. Every time I lay down to sleep, I was afraid someone would come in my door. Finally, a lot of little children did come in and they all had dolls. It became chaos in my quarters. I heard someone outside mention your name and I could not figure out why you would not come to us. I was trying to get some people out of the room so I could lock the door. I was afraid I would never get any sleep-then two men came through the door carrying stove pipes, the kind they used years ago when installing room heaters. They proceeded through the room without stopping and opened another door which I didn't even know existed-and went down to the basement. I then realized the door had no lock and there was no way to prevent somebody coming up from the basement into my room. All of a sudden I looked in a corner and saw a man whom I did not know, crouched on the floor and waking up. It was some-body I had never seen, so I asked him what he was doing there.

"Oh, I sleep here all the time." "Well, I want you to get out of here." "No, I've got to shave first." I was still afraid those two men, who were from Iraq, would come back into my room with that weird animal they had. I then looked out the window and exclaimed: "Thank the Lord, its daylight."

4:05 a.m. I had been awake about five minutes when things began to happen. If you are wondering why I was awake at that hour-it was not too unusual-I have insomnia and quite often I'm awake at that hour. Sometimes I go back to sleep and sometimes I just lie there until daybreak. The pill doesn't work every time.

At any rate, there I was lying peacefully-waiting for day to break. Then I heard something from the other side that I had heard many times before. It was Annie's voice-she was beginning to mutter softly, but I knew that softness wouldn't last long. It would get louder and louder, soon reaching a crescendo. It usually doesn't take long for this to happen-and it didn't. Then the ritual of kicking began. Oftentimes in these episodes I yell at her, "Annie, stop that kicking." In this instance I decide to do nothing-just lie there and let my shins take the punishment. If she breaks my leg bone or pounds my flesh until it turns blue-so be it!

In these nightmares her words are never distinguishable, so I never know exactly what's going on in her mind. The kicking becomes more vicious and the screaming begins. It's difficult to describe a scream, but I would liken hers to that of a female being violated or maybe being beaten with a lead pipe. The kicking and screaming stop and she bolts upright-looks around and lies back down-waiting for arrival of another dream.

"Annie, what was happening to you this morning about four o'clock?"

"Well, I had another one of those dreams and I was horrified. Someone was cutting lights on and I couldn't figure out how he got into the house. When he got to our bedroom he had a flashlight and began shining it in my face. I kept trying to say 'Who is it?'-but words wouldn't come-I guess I was too scared to talk. I was actually awake enough to know that you were in bed with me, so I started kicking you to wake you up. The way I was kicking-you're probably all bruised up. I finally sat up in bed and saw you there, and the other guy was gone. Ray, I honestly believe if I had not seen you there, I would have had a heart attack. I have never been more afraid than last night."

How come we see more and more TV commercials depicting restroom scenes? Sometimes I feel like if I see another one I'll puke.

And speaking of restrooms, manufacturers of accessories attached to walls therein must have the greatest salesmen in the world on their payroll.

Years ago, when our country was in the midst of an energy crunch, those guys were successful in talking what seemed to be ninety percent of establishments into installing new type hand dryers. They were electric. All we had to do was push a button and hot air would burst forth, drying our hands as we rubbed them together, kind of like baseball players do before grabbing their bat. I could have dried my hands ten times as fast with the old style paper towels. Most times hands were not dry after the first push and we had to hit the button again. Can you imagine how much energy we wasted by using millions of those things across our country daily?

Most places I enter now have replaced them with nice paper dispensers from which you can hit a lever and get all the paper you want. I even saw one the other day that dispensed a towel upon moving my hands in front of an opening. If technology people can do that, why can't they make better shingles, locks and carpets?

Another thing those salesmen were proficient at was convincing those establishments to install new and expensive gadgets to dispense toilet tissue. They devised more ways to make it accessible to us than there are to skin a cat.

The most expensive looking and most ridiculous one is that big black round job that dispenses paper in the shape of a rope, which you have to unravel before using. I don't know how much that thing cost, but it's not as efficient as the old style wood roller type that probably sells for about 79 cents in these inflated times. Unfortunately, many establishments are still using those behemoths.

Notable Quotables

#1-There seems to be increased interest in baseball-and even softball-these days. It seems as soon as kids get big enough to swing a bat there's a place for them in the game. I believe real action begins with a game called "T-ball". It's played without a pitcher. A ball is placed on top of a flexible pedestal and the kids step up and take a swing at it. When the kids hit it in fair territory they run the bases in the usual manner.

On this particular day Mary was a newcomer-her very first game. Her first two swings resulted in foul balls, but on her third swing she made solid contact and the ball got through the infield for a solid hit. She immediately dropped the bat and ran, but not toward first base. She ran directly from home plate to second base! Inasmuch as she hadn't touched first base, the player who finally retrieved the ball touched Mary with it, who was called out because she had never touched first base.

Dejectedly, she trotted back to the team bench and held her head down.

Coach: "Mary, why in the world did you run to second instead of first base?"

Mary: "Because everybody I saw run to first base got out."

#2-And this is good. A friend of mine was recently in a dental lab waiting for his upper plate to be adjusted.

While sitting there he saw an elderly gentleman come in, carrying a brown bag. He approached the receptionist's desk and spoke to the attendant.

"I'm bringing this in for my wife." He reached in the bag and brought out a lower denture plate which had two missing teeth. "Last night she was eating a hamburger and two of the front teeth fell out-and need to be replaced." He reached into the bag one more time and brought out a single tooth." Here's one of the teeth. You'll have to wait a couple of days for the other one."

Communication

Since the beginning of time humans have had a need to communicate with each other, and it has been accomplished in a number of ways.

One of the ways American Indians used was to send smoke signals from hilltop to hilltop.

And I'm amazed at how deaf people are able to communicate with each other simply by movement of fingers.

I don't know when the first letter was written, or who wrote it, but when the practice caught on, it flourished in a hurry.

After letters made their appearance, it became necessary to find a way to deliver them in a timely manner. In the days of the Old

West the Pony Express did a pretty good job of delivering written messages on time, during the short period in which it existed. In fact, it probably could have delivered a letter from Charlotte, NC to Kinston, NC in less time than it sometimes takes for the USPS to do it in this day and time, which is three to six days.

With all the modern methods of communication available today, there are probably many people who have never written a letter-and it's refreshing to me when I run across one that I consider unique. I have recently run across two that fall in that category.

I discovered a short time ago through research that my great grandfather-on the Rouse side of my tree-was killed during the Civil War while serving in the Confederate Army, the date of death being May 3, 1863.

Private James F. Jones had been wounded in the battle of Malvern Hill, a spot on the map between Richmond and Petersburg, Virginia, July 1, 1862. He was allowed to return to his home in Greene County, NC to recuperate.

After a period of recuperation he walked back to his unit in Virginia. On February 12, 1863, he wrote his last letter. He was killed in the Battle of Chancellorsville, Virginia, May 3, 1863. There were so many dead soldiers to be buried, that instead of digging separate graves, a big hole was dug and the bodies were thrown in it together.

He had entered military service at age 26, April 25, 1861. I consider this letter, the original of which is in the hands of William

A. Jones, a descendant, to be of great historical significance to our family.

An almost indistinguishable photo of the letter follows. Below it are the printed words of the letter in full.

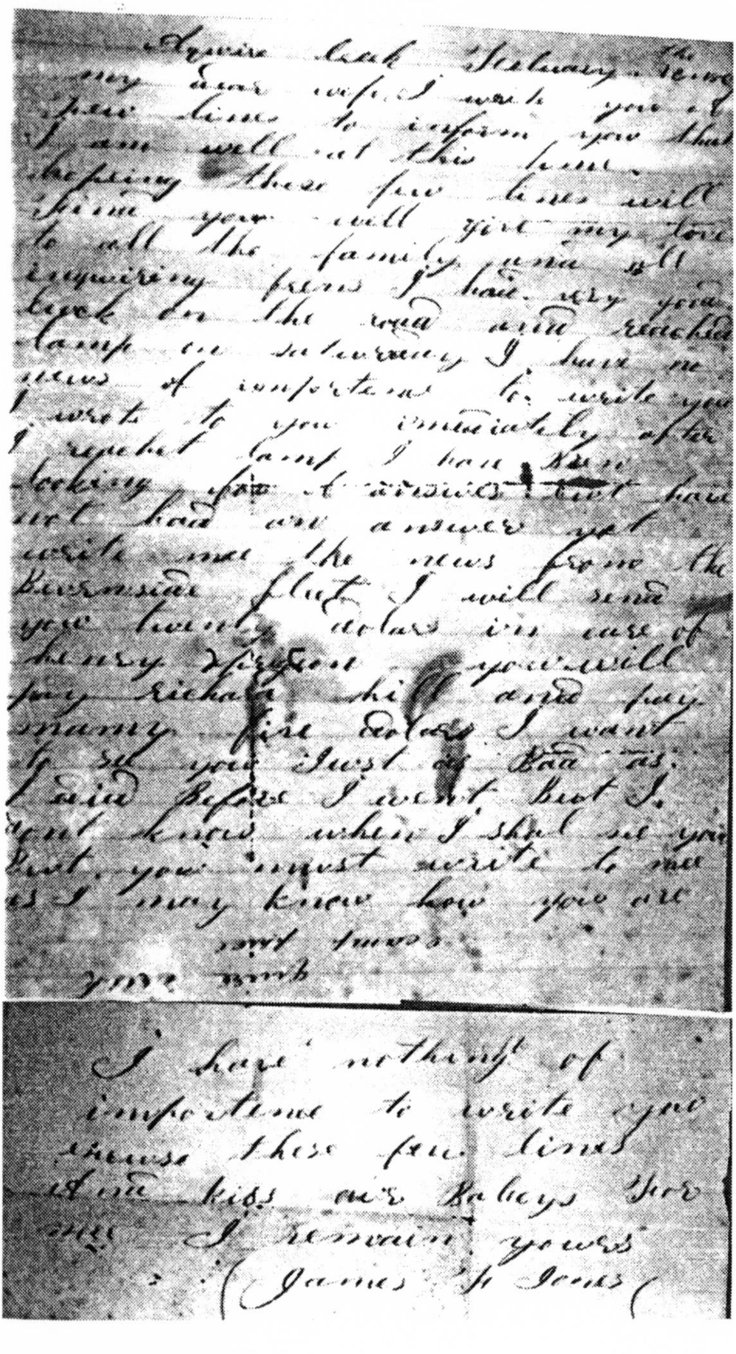

Squire Creek

Feb. 12, 1863

My dear wife:

I write you a few lines to inform you that I am well at this time. Hoping these few lines will find you well. Give my love to all the family and all inquiring friends. I had very good luck on the road and reached camp on Saturday. I have no news of importance to write you. I wrote to you immediately after I reached camp. I have been looking for a answer but have not had an answer yet. Write me the news from the Burnside fleet. I will send you $20 in care of Henry Pridgen. You will pay Richard Hill and pay Mammy $5. I want to see you just as bad as before I went but I don't know when I shall see you, but you must write to me as I may know how you are. I have nothing of importance to write you excuse these few lines and kiss our babys for me. I remain yours.

James F. Jones

The other letter is of very recent vintage, but is also held in high esteem by me. It was written by our youngest grandchild, Katherine Demianiuk, who just turned eight.

The family visited us for a couple of weeks, but the father, Ed, had to return home early-while the remainder of the family remained with us. They drove to Greenville-about twenty five miles from Kinston, and on the way there she wrote the following message to her dad while occupying the back seat of the car. "Floyd" refers to the family dog.

Katherine has recently entered the world of softball and is currently batgirl for her older sister's school softball team. She has already decided she wants to be a pitcher, and her "pichis" refer to the good practice pitches she made one day after Ed left Kinston; I think the writing gives an interesting insight as to what goes on in the minds of little children.

Below the photo of the original letter are the printed words in full that might be easier to decipher.

Hi DAD,   5/15/06

I am going to De Breef aunt eleneer
Camp to visit and i got tew
Reading Books and a coloring
Book tell floyd i said Hi! tow
mepes milk Bones have you
and floyd eaten? and thare gos
floyd to Dieet... have you eaten
more sence we have Been Gone
or have you Been eating Less sence
we are gone? I hope you and
floyd are doing good tell
floyd that i saw a Hot dog
do g yester day i miss you and floyd
in a row and about 5 good pichis
pichis i a day now
we are on are way to greer
vill and today we are gai's
to dixey queen and in a
few days we are going
to coldincral and i will
see JP, Piann, and uncl Mike
i gess i will see you
wen i get home Bie Love you
Katie

8/15/06

Hi Dad,

I am going to be breef aunt eleneer came to visit and I go two reading books and a coloring book tell floyd I said hi! how meney milk bones have you and floyd eaten? and thare gos floyd's diet!!!!! have you eaten more sence we have been gone or have you been eating less sence we are gone? i hope you and Floyd are doing good tell floyd that i saw a Hot Dog dog yester day i miss you and floyd I got 5 good pichis in a row and about 18 good pichis i a day. now we are on our way to greenville and today we are gong to dixey queen and in a few days we are going to goldincral and i will see JP, Diann, and uncl Mike I gess I will see you wen i get home Bie love you

Katie

The Pie

All of you church folks out there are familiar with the get-togethers most churches have occasionally at which we meet, eat, and chat.

Some congregations refer to them as potluck dinners. Some call them covered dish meals, others-picnics on the grounds.

Call them what you may-they are all essentially the same. They entail the taking of a plate or bowl of food of your choice to be placed on tables along which buffet lines are formed-and one can partake of his or her favorite dish. Down south that means such favorite things as collard greens and chicken and pastry, as well as a multitude of other delicacies. And one thing is an absolute must at all of these events; there must be an adequate supply of fried chicken.

Those events also become a showplace for desserts, which are placed on a separate table where diners can walk at a very slow pace and choose the most delectable looking item, or items, they can spot. One can choose from coconut cakes, carrot cakes, chocolate cakes, pineapple cakes, pound cakes, and an assortment of pies.

The ladies of the church take great pride in preparing their desserts to be displayed and consumed by a ravenous gathering.

A few weeks ago Northwest Christian Church kicked off its celebration of the year of jubilee, our fiftieth year of existence. The evening's event was to end with a covered dish supper.

Carolyn, our church secretary, decided she wanted to be a part of the celebration by baking her favorite recipe, a deep dish apple pie, but not one of those shallow ones you can purchase at the supermarket for two or three bucks. Hers would be of the higher caliber Mrs. Smith variety-those thick jobs with lots of fruit.

So, shortly after noon on the day of the event, she begins her preparations. She feels good and enters her venture with excitement and courage. She reads the recipe over and over, even though she's cooked it many times previously. She will not be hasty. She makes sure every measurement is done correctly and every pinch is of the exact magnitude called for.

When everything is prepared according to the recipe, she then pours the ingredients into the deep dish crust and levels the mixture perfectly. When she's satisfied with this procedure, she gently lays the top crust over the mixture, making sure it is perfectly level-with no imperfections.

It's time to open the oven door and gently place that delicacy on a rack, making sure it is carried there in a perfect uniform manner. She performs this exercise famously and closes the oven door and sets the timer.

The timer bell clangs and she gently opens the oven. Has the crust fallen? Has it over-cooked? No. No. The crust has turned to a golden tan and is perfectly shaped. Apples are all contained. It looks to be the most perfect pie Carolyn Tyson has every produced. It will rival Mrs. Smith's-and Mrs. Smith makes great pies.

She carefully extracts the pan from the oven and places it on the kitchen table to cool. This ritual is performed with dexterity, again not wanting to disturb the ingredients in any way.

Soon the time arrives for her to transport the subject from her home to the kitchen at Northwest Church. There it would be placed on a table beside other entries in the unofficial competition to see which lady bakes the best pie. This pie looked good enough to lift her to great heights of esteem among Northwest cooks. Perhaps even allow her to be named Queen of Cuisine at the institution of worship. She would show those ladies something! A smile crossed her pretty face. Inside she began acquiring a feeling of pride and accomplishment for a job well done. She had been presented with a challenge and she had met it!

The only thing left for her to do is to transport the item safely to Northwest-not a big deal. She places the pie pan on the front seat of the car, close to her, where it will be safe. She turns the switch key and the motor starts and runs smoothly-no vibration. She takes her foot off the brake pedal and shifts it to the accelerator pedal and gently depresses it. She wants no sudden stops or starts. She's going to give this pie a lot of TLC on its way to the church. She's going to show those other ladies what a perfectly cooked deep dish apple pie looks like. She begins to wonder who the lucky eight people will be who get the chance to partake of her choice dessert.

She exits her driveway without mishap and takes the road which will take her to hwy 58 and on to Kinston. She is not the possessor of a single care in the whole world. No feeling of discombobulation.

Do you remember those seven words of an old song that say: "Into each life some rain must fall?" Well, as she approaches that eight sided sign at the entrance to the highway, the sky is clear blue, but she is about to be the victim of a deluge.

As she approaches the sign, she lifts her foot from the "A" pedal to the "B" pedal and depresses it very lightly in order to initiate a gradual stop. Doesn't work. Brakes grab! The law of inertia kicks in.

The car stops. Carolyn stops. The pie pan doesn't stop. It keeps its forward motion. Then there is a sound! Not a really loud one. Not like a replay of the "big bang". Not like the roaring clash of cymbals or the sharp clap of thunder. It is not like the sound of a Civil War cannon. Not even like the sound of a pop-gun in the hands of a kid. It's the dull sound of a thud-just a simple old thud emanating from the floorboard on the passenger side, but it's devastating to Carolyn. She is frozen motionless in her seat for a few seconds that seem to be a lifetime. She suspects the worst-and she gets it. When she gets around to the act of moving her head, she looks upon a mass of food-stuff crumbled a short distance to the right of her feet.

It has no resemblance whatever to a ribbon-winning deep dish apple pie. It is pure mush-nothing more. Eight people will not be coming up to her with congratulations on baking the best deep dish apple pie they have ever consumed.

No. Humans would never have the opportunity to appreciate the delicacy of that once beautiful piece of culinary art consisting of freshly baked fruit lying between perfectly cooked upper and bottom crusts.

But-Carolyn decides her venture will not be a total loss. The pie will be eaten! One picture is worth more than a thousand words!

CHAPTER NINE
LIFE IS—DISAPPOINTMENTS

Inasmuch as I've already declared that life is not a bowl of cherries-just what is it? Webster furnishes us with more than a dozen definitions of the word. The one I am most impressed with is this: "It is all that is experienced by an individual during his existence." In other words, every decision we make, every conversation we participate in, every game we play or witness-all are part of life. It is also a series of events that lead to happiness or sorrow, jubilation or dismay, wealth or poverty, sickness or wellness. And it is a sequence of happenings that can change our quality of existence in the wink of an eye.

For most of us, I believe successes outnumber disappointments, which make for happier lives-but all of us do suffer some failed expectations.

One of my early disappointments occurred when I was a high school sophomore. I was a skinny kid, mostly skin and bones, but I liked to participate in playground football with neighborhood friends. I decided to try out for the football team at Grainger High School. With all that heavy protective paraphernalia on, I must have weighed about 120. It was not the most desirable weight to withstand the rigors of that most physical sport. I survived the tryout period without mishap and didn't think I had done too poorly. When the varsity members were chosen, however, Ray Rouse was among the missing. That was probably the biggest disappointment of my student life.

*   *   *

As would be expected, disappointments suffered by sports teams are probably as prevalent as in any group of people. The most glaring recent one was absorbed by the Chicago Cubs baseball team.

The team hasn't won a World Series since 1908 and hasn't been National League Champions since 1945. They have been champions of their division a total of three times since that date, the most recent success occurring just three years ago, 2003. Of all their failures, perhaps this last one was the most frustrating-they came so close to winning.

The team played well and became champions of the Central Division of the National League. Cub fans from the Atlantic to the

Pacific were ecstatic. Was this the year the boys in Chicago would make it to the World Series again? Would this be the year they would shed the shackles that had held them captive for so long? Reaching their goal would not be easy. Perennial division winners-the Atlanta Braves-were blocking their path.

Fortunately, for the Cubbies, the Braves played poorly-as had become their custom in playoffs-and the Cubs won and advanced to the National League Championship Series. Things looked good for Chicago. The Cubs' return to a World Series for the first time in fifty-eight years seemed genuinely possible.

In the League Championship Series against the Florida Marlins, Chicago lost the first game, in spite of playing in their famed Wrigley Field. They won the next two games and Cub fans were beside themselves. Things looked even brighter when their team won the next game to go up 3-1 in the seven game series. Chicago was on a roll. Needed just one more game, but they lost to the Marlins in a 4-0 shut out. Their lead was trimmed to 3-2, but they returned to their beloved Wrigley and fully expected to win game #4 and become a participant in the World Series.

Didn't happen. They were leading three runs to none-just five outs away from the big show when the roof caved in. Due to a series of bizarre plays the Cubs lost the game. Series tied at 3-3. After blowing that game, the Cubs never had a chance in the seventh and deciding game. Even with their star pitcher on the mound, they were beaten by a score of 9-6. Cub fans had been through many trials and tribulations in their quest for a place at the table of a World Series, but it was not to be in the year 2003. It had to be their greatest disappointment.

*   *   *

For many, life is a little like being on a roller coaster, being atop a hill one moment and in a valley the next. The US Space Program has been just such a project. Not too long after the end of World War II the United States and Russia became engaged in a race to determine who would be first to conquer space.

Russia became the first to put an artificial satellite into space in October 1957. The US put its first satellite up four months later, January 31, 1958. The race was on.

A race to reach the moon ensued. Many experimental exercises were required in preparation for man to achieve the goal that had been only a dream heretofore. It was in that preparatory period that the US had its first major setback to the project. It occurred in 1967 at Cape Canaveral when three astronauts died in a flash fire that erupted in the spaceship while they were waiting for liftoff. That disappointment was overcome in 1969, when America landed a man on the moon.

The next moon mission was another disappointment. It had to be aborted due to a problem with oxygen flow.

That turned out to be minor, however, compared to a really great disaster that occurred January 28, 1986.

The seven member crew, including one female school teacher, lifted off from Cape Canaveral-witnessed by millions around the world via television. In no time at all after being lifted from the earth's surface, the rocket and shuttle became engulfed in flame and exploded. Thousands of pieces of metal and human bodies were scattered across the Florida waters below. The tragedy occurred because something called O-rings had failed to do their job under extremely cold conditions.

That was the biggest disappointment NASA had ever suffered, but it re-grouped and went on to further successes, having learned from their failure.

*　　　*　　　*

Yes, disappointments are part of our everyday life. All of us suffer through them. At the time of this writing, one of the great sports spectacles that occur in this country annually is in progress-the NCAA Basketball Championship. This extravaganza has become the biggest sports event of the year.

The tournament begins with sixty-five of the nation's best teams competing. Some sports fans will say there are only 64 teams-not 65-there are actually 65 each year. Teams # 64 and 65, play each other in the very first game to determine which will be eliminated, in order to reduce the number to an even 64. Within three days the number is pared down to 32. That number is reduced to 16 after two more days of play. The number is then reduced to 8, 4, and finally 2. At that point 63 teams have suffered disappointments by being defeated. On the tournaments final day only one team will have survived the tournament without the disappointment of losing a game.

Most of us sports fans have a favorite team we root for. Sometimes we can get so caught up in our enthusiasm for that team that we suffer with the players when they lose. We might even suffer more. The players know they probably will not win every game and learn to take losses in stride-but attempt to do better next time out. On the other hand, we expect them to win every game. We don't want any disappointments from our team.

*   *   *

When we think of missed opportunities and disappointments in our country's history, we cannot omit military leaders, the greatest of which-in my opinion-was George Washington.

This young man, who later would become commander-in-chief of America's military forces in the American Revolutionary War, first suffered disappointing defeats during the French and Indian war.

At age twenty-three, he held the rank of Lieutenant Colonel in the British forces when he suffered the disappointment of surrendering to a larger French and American Indian force. A fort he had built for protection had turned out to be inadequate, forcing the surrender.

A year later he also suffered defeat in the Battle of Monongahela, in which he was aide to the British General who was commanding the forces.

The defeats and successes he experienced in the French and Indian War would serve him well in later years as commander-in-chief of the Continental Army during the American Revolution that lasted from 1774-1783.

Washington assumed command of the forces on July 3, 1775. Early in the war he lost a number of important battles, including the battle for New York and the battle of Long Island.

At one point he had suffered so many defeats that the future of his rag-tag army was in doubt, but he was resilient. He rolled with the punches and was endowed with a determination to win. The war's direction of events turned in Washington's favor when the French became an ally in 1778.

Facts indicate that Washington actually lost more battles than he won, but he had attributes to help win freedom from the greatest empire of that time. He possessed the know-how to keep his army intact, even in the face of defeat. He had the perseverance to wear the British down over the long haul. He knew how to exploit mistakes made by the enemy.

Yes, he had his share of disappointments, but he didn't let them overwhelm him, and his resolve resulted in the creation of this great free country of ours.

*   *   *

When we talk about disappointments among specific groups of people, we can not omit politicians. That group of people, who run for office, hoping for prestige or financial rewards, is huge in this country, and most of those who choose to run are eventually disappointed in the results.

I think of President Jimmy Carter, whose official name is James Earl Carter.

Having been practically unknown outside the state of Georgia, he entered the fray for presidency of the United States as a Democrat. He defeated Gerald R. Ford in the November 1975 general election-being installed as head man of the White House in January 1976.

Like most incoming presidents, he inherited multiple problems. During his tenure the country faced high inflation, which led him to put in place gasoline price controls in 1977. He was also architect of Airline Deregulation Act in 1978. And he signed, along with fourteen other nations, a treaty that was designed to stop the proliferation of nuclear weapons. He also did his part in enlarging the federal government by creating a Department of Energy. And he was author of a treaty that would ultimately turn control of the Panama Canal over to Panama. Possibly his greatest accomplishment was negotiating the Camp David Accords between Israel and Egypt.

The last half of Carter's term was fraught with foreign policy situations.

In 1979, the American Embassy in Tehran was overrun by militants. They took sixty-six hostages and used them as pawns to force America to return the Shah of Iran from exile in this country back to Iran. This was refused by Carter. A small handful of hostages were released, but fifty-two were held for more than a year.

An attempt to rescue the hostages was made, but it was unsuccessful. That failed attempt did a lot of damage to the popularity of President Carter. Due to his declining popularity, he lost his bid for reelection to Ronald Reagan, the Republican candidate.

His defeat at the poles by American voters was a great disappointment to Jimmy Carter-and it was obvious. I recall his wife later saying how much they regretted leaving the White House after only one term.

Even though he was disappointed, Carter was not devastated. He was a person of high morals and character. In his farewell speech in January 1981, he stated that he was leaving the office of presidency to once again become an ordinary citizen. But he became more-he became an extraordinary one.

He immediately embarked on a career to become a true international humanitarian. He has worked to improve the lives of those living in poor countries. He has tackled and solved numerous problems in countries that others deemed unsolvable. He has been very visible in his help to construct houses for Habitat for Humanity, allowing that organization to become a worldwide success.

Yes, Jimmy Carter was the recipient of a great disappointment in being defeated for a second term, but he chose to overcome it by becoming deeply involved in charity work, mediating disputes around the world, writing and lecturing. He has probably achieved more success in his life after his presidency than he did in the White House.

*   *   *

Nations, also, suffer disappointments-and the greatest one in our country's history was most assuredly the Vietnam War. War was never declared, so many people referred to it as a "conflict". Talk to any of the participants of it, however, and you will come away knowing they had been involved in a WAR! And it was a hellish one-not like any other our nation had been involved in.

Not only did it take the lives of at least 50,000 American servicemen, more than 200,000 became disabled. The affair also cost US taxpayers more than $150,000,000,000. Yes, that figure is one hundred fifty billion dollars. From its beginning in the 1950's no one ever imagined it would last for seventeen years.

Like most wars, it was a political thing. It could be called an off-shoot of the "cold war" that had existed between our country and the USSR since shortly after the end of World War II, in which the two countries had been allies. Russia was intent on spreading its communist type government across the world and the US was intent on stopping it.

Our government took the stance that it would support,militarily, if need be-any country that would defy takeover by communist elements. We would do this even when that country was controlled by a corrupt government. The US felt that if one country in an area should succumb to communism, others would follow, creating what would become known as the Domino Theory.

The fracas actually had its beginning in-not Vietnam-but Laos, its neighbor. It spilled over into Vietnam, which was split between two factions: the pro-communists in the north and the pro-west in the southern half of the country.

In November 1963, President John Kennedy was assassinated and Lyndon B. Johnson became commander-in-chief. It was in his administration that the US greatly increased its aid to South Vietnam, including the sending of combat troops to become actively involved in the undeclared war of Vietnam.

Things did not go well for us and after several years of fighting, disenchantment began spreading across the country for the war. More and more Americans became disillusioned with the war-one that seemed to have no end.

A military draft, similar to one used in World War II, was activated. Quite a few of those whose number was drawn chose not to report for duty. Instead, they fled to Canada to avoid active duty in Vietnam.

Our troops were fighting gallantly on the ground, but were meeting stiff resistance from North Vietnam troops. They couldn't tell friend from foe. Also, Americans were not used to jungle warfare, where the enemy would attack in open spaces and then run back into the jungle-where they had crude, but effective, booby-traps awaiting anyone who followed.

More and more pressure was being put on by the US populace to get out of Vietnam. This finally resulted in a peace agreement being signed in January 1973. Both sides announced they had won the war.

The last American advisors left Vietnam on March 15, 1973. The war, that was not a war, ended for American troops at that time. American troops had fought valiantly in a no-win situation. Not winning was something new for America. I don't know of anything we had gained in that seventeen years. It was a great disappointment to our government, but it must have been an even greater disappointment to our troops who were not welcomed home as heroes, as soldiers in past wars had been-despite their tremendous sacrifices for their country.

*   *   *

What can we do to put those disappointments behind us? If you're talking sports, you need to shake them off like water runs off a duck's back. Tell yourself as you leave the scene of battle that it was just a game-and start preparing yourself for the next one.

But whatever the disappointment relates to-whether it be sports, elections, marital relations, or whatever-we should remember that God is still in his palatial home, earth is in its proper place and the sun will rise tomorrow. It will be another day.

CHAPTER TEN
LIFE IS — ME

nnie Swinson Phillips and I were married in 1947 in what I would describe as a "nondescript" wedding. A small thing at the preacher's house. Total number of people present was seven: Reverend Phillips (no relation), Annie's siblings-Eleanor and Bill, James and Ruby Boone and the two of us.

Total cost of the wedding was ten dollars-five for the license and five for the preacher. The whole affair took no more than five minutes. That's why I described it as nondescript.

We had decided beforehand that we would not have children for a few years, which turned out to be eight. We wanted to have a good time by traveling, which we figured we wouldn't be able to do after children arrived. So, in that respect, the first eight years of our married life was not typical of that of most other young couples. My job paid me $160 per month. Annie earned $20 per week. We had no other source of income, but were able to save enough to take a nice trip out of state each year.

Annie gave birth to Mike exactly eight years later, right on schedule. Four years afterward, also as planned, Cindy arrived. That completed our family number at four, as we also desired.

The next couple of decades were somewhat different from the first eight years. We became a one income family and we had the usual struggles of a young family. No more long, extended vacations. We spent my income buying groceries and clothes, paying doctor bills, utilities and the likes. In due time, like most of our friends, we bought a lot and had a house constructed, which turned out to be a duplex. In later years, we would construct two more houses. Those family years were a struggle, but were good ones.

Both children completed their higher education on time and left home to seek careers of their own. Cindy and Ed are living in Monroe, Wisconsin, and are the parents of two girls and a son. All is well there.

Mike now makes his home in Asheville, NC, with Helen and two step-children. All is well there.

After the kids moved out, things became better from a financial standpoint. We found that maintaining a home for two was much less expensive than that for four, enabling us to save some money once again. Another period of our life had expired. Within a few years we were ready for another-that of retirement.

My partner and I sold our insurance agency when I was age 62. I hung around the new business full time for a couple of years and then on a part time basis until my 70th birthday. That was when I entered full retirement and our love for traveling returned.

I believe the best period of time for us must have been in the 1980's, when some very enjoyable events occurred-the most memorable one being a seven week cross-country trip by automobile. Eleanor accompanied us on the journey that included a three day cruise up the inside passage from Vancouver, British Columbia, to Skagway, Alaska. We viewed some of the most beautiful scenery there is in the USA and Canada. Distance in miles traveled was more than halfway around the earth. What a wonderful trip. That was 1987.

The very next month after we returned, on August 21, 22, and 23, another enjoyable event occurred. It was the anniversary celebration of the Grainger High School class of 1942-the 45th.

We had classmates coming in from Arizona, Texas, Georgia, Virginia, Florida, New Mexico, and Maryland-maybe even other states. We had convened once before, five years earlier, but there were some at this one whom I hadn't seen in forty five years-and they looked good.

Charles Brown did a masterful job as Master of Ceremonies and a grand time was had by all-we even had a video made of the entire event. Sadly, we learned that our original group of ninety had been reduced by seventeen through efforts of the Grim Reaper.

*   *   *

Charlie asked me if I would try to come up with a little some-thing to share with the class that would consume a few minutes of program time. Just anything I wanted to present.

What I came up with might qualify as a poem, because it does contain some rhythmical composition. What it actually turned out to be was a thumbnail sketch of my life from age six to sixty-three. If it turned out to be "something" in Brown's opinion, I don't know.

At any rate, it became my first attempt at any kind of writing-and I wasn't the target of any thrown food left over from the evening dinner.

High school graduations are, as a rule, rather insignificant events, except for those involved in them. Ours of 1942, however, was significant-not only to the class and the little City of Kinston, NC-but to the entire United States of America. That class, like thousands of others across the country that year, was the first high school grad-uation of America's youth during World War II. It would set a trend in our country that would last forever. That conflict, referred to by some as the last "Good War", resulted in sixteen million Americans being garbed in military uniforms to help defeat tyrants who aspired to control the world.

Lives of the '42 class would be forever changed, as would the lives of most Americans, beyond that day in June. Those of us who didn't seek higher education found ourselves in military service within months. Others made it through college freshman class before being called to duty as warriors. I was drafted in January, 1943, but my fellow classmate, Charles Brown, didn't go in until a year later, because he was one year younger.

This drain on the country's male force opened up a whole new opportunity for the country's female population. It began matriculating to large cities to take over defense jobs being vacated by men entering the armed forces. Rosie, the secretary, became Rosie, the riveter. Women discovered they could build airplanes, ships, and tanks, in addition to having babies and cooking-and they liked it.

As for classmates of 1942, we scattered hither and yon, of necessity. We traveled to places of which we had never heard, and sailed the seven seas.

Less than half the class returned to pick up their lives in Kinston after the war. Some, of course, hadn't survived the conflict, having their lives terminated on foreign soil-one being killed in his first day of combat.

Yes, the war had a huge impact on the Grainger High Class of 1942 and on the entire American populace, as well. The lives of most of our class members would be drastically different had the war not occurred. No longer was it a given that Dick would marry Jane, his childhood sweetheart, even though it still happened occasionally. Many would not seek their livelihood locally. I can think of Ellis, who married a girl from Texas and settled in San Antonio after a career in military service; Ernest, who married and made his home in Henderson, NC; Gillikin, who domiciled in Georgia as a physician; Walter, who spent the war as a nuclear scientist in Los Alamos, New Mexico, and decided to remain there. Gordon spent the remainder of his life as a pediatrician in Lakeland, Fla. Reynolds spent most of his remaining life as a dentist in Fayetteville, NC. Jean moved to Camarilla, Ca. Pete and Bill habitated in Miami-living just a few blocks from each other. Otis achieved the rank of General in the US Army and remained in the Pacific Region until his death a few years ago. Ed King settled in Raleigh, NC, Ed Grady in Columbia, SC, and O'Steen in Virginia. Sally settled in Raleigh, NC and Jane in New Bern, NC. These are just a few of our classmates who found that life could be lived abundantly outside the environs of Lenoir County, NC.

Who in the class of 1942, on that day in June, could have predicted the future course of events for us individually, as a group, or for our country, itself?

Toast to Friendship

"Friendship is a chain of gold

Shaped in God's all perfect mold,

Each link a smile, a laugh, a tear,

A clasp of the hand, a world of cheer,

As steadfast as the ages roll

Binding closer, soul to soul.

No matter how far or heavy the load

Sweet is the journey on friendships road."

—Anonymous

Lots of things usually happened at high school reunions. It's easy to have fun there. You see people you haven't seen nor heard from since graduation. Some you recognize, some you don't. You find out how many spouses everybody has had. You find out who's bald and who's not. How much weight has everyone put on? You find out where everybody lives.

You also hear a lot of jokes from the MC. I just ran across a few that were tossed out on our fiftieth. I'll give you a sampling of them, some of which are still in existence. It seems like old jokes never die-they just float around. These are some of my favorites.

1-This guy had never traveled outside his county, but in a raffle he won a trip to New York City. A lady neighbor found out about it and she asked Jim if he would look up her son, whose name was John Dunn, and asked him to get in touch with her. Jim asked her what his phone number was. She said, "I don't know, I've never called him." He asked her what the son's address was and she answered, "I don't know. I have not heard from him in years. All I know is, he's in New York."

When Jim got to New York he had no idea how to locate John, but he really wanted to help his neighbor, so he began walking the streets asking pedestrians if they knew John Dunn. All answers were negative.

Finally, after entering the financial district, he saw a sign that said Dunn and Bradstreet. Jim immediately entered the building and saw a lady at a desk and asked, "Do you have a John here?" "Yes, second door on your right down the hall." As Jim approached the door, he saw a man coming out of the men's room. He went up to him and asked, "Are you Dunn?" The fellow answered in the affirmative, upon which Jim said, "Call your mom."

2-A highway patrolman stopped a driver and the driver asked him, "What are you stopping me for?" "I'm giving you a ticket for speeding." "I was not speeding, I was going 55. You can't write me a ticket. I won't sign it. I've got my rights like everybody else has." The patrolman looked at the man's wife and asked, "Ma'am, does he give you this kind of trouble at home?" "No, officer, not to me, I learned a long time ago not to argue with him when he's drunk."

3-A city preacher retired and went into a rural area and bought a few acres. He had envied farmers who seemed to have a lot of time on their hands, so he decided he wanted to try raising a few chickens. He went to town and bought 100 chicks. The next week he bought 100 more. Another trip and another 100 chicks. On a fourth trip for another 100 the store clerk said to him, "You must be going into the chicken business in a big way." "Well, I wanted to, but I must be doing something wrong. I'm either planting them too deep or watering them too much."

4-One of the many memory jokes: An 80 year old man was sitting on a park bench one day when a park policeman came by. The old man was crying so hard that tears had puddled at his feet. The cop asked, "What's wrong, old fellow? I've seen people cry, but this is ridiculous." The old man answered, "I've got a 24 year old wife at home. She's beautiful, she's a gourmet cook, she's madly in love with me, and is patiently waiting for me right now." "So, what's the problem, old man?" His answer: "I can't remember where I live."

5-In a western town back in the 1800's an old whiskered prospector came to town on a mule. Out of the saloon came a cowboy who had a few drinks too many. He went over to the prospector and asked, "Hey, you old codger, do you know how to dance?" "No, says the prospector." "Well, I'm going to teach you." He pulled out his six-shooter and shot just in front of the old man's feet. The prospector counted the shots-1, 2, 3, 4, 5, 6. He knew the drunk's gun was empty. He went over to his mule, pulled his shotgun out and stuck the barrel in the cowboy's face and asked, "Have you ever kissed a mule?" Cowboy, after a minutes hesitation, "No, but I've always wanted to."

*   *   *

At our fiftieth each of us received something I'll bet no one else ever did. Jean P. Booth was our principal when we graduated in 1942. He was still living in 1992 and was a guest of honor at our festivities. He presented each student a second diploma, but words were different from the ones imprinted on the original parchment. The words on my new one read thusly: "This congratulatory diploma certifies that Ray P. Rouse has honorably aspired and attained a geriatric plateau of 50 years, and from this vantage point, is entitled to view all honors and privileges of the "New Age" Geriatric Fraternity."

This 30th day of May, 1992.

It was personally signed in the inimitable handwriting like none other I've ever seen. Truly, J. P. Booth was a great educator and a wonderful person.

*   *   *

Someone had saved a copy of the school paper that was printed November 12, 1941, and each was given a copy. I notice the cost of each issue was 6 cents. It was named the Ki-Hi. I noticed that Doris Bradshaw was named junior member of the business and professional women's club for the month of November. Great selection. Doris attended all our reunions and I still see her regularly, since we are members of the same church. I also saw where Lois Wooten-remember the "tackler"-was named "Who's Who" for the same month.

There is also a photo of the football team of 21 members. Two of those shown there were killed in World War II.

Among other old paraphernalia I found in my "stuff" was a faded page torn from a Reader's Digest of long ago that contained the following quip: Sign in store window-"Any faulty merchandise will be cheerfully replaced with merchandise of equal quality."

Another thing I found was a weathered perfect attendance certificate that was issued June 2, 1942, certifying that Ray Rouse had attended the entire school term without being absent or tardy. I thought I had done <u>something</u> right during my school experience.

In doing a little digging, I found that in 1942 our city public school enrollment was 3,314. At the time of our last reunion, the number was only 4,554. In 1942, there were 104 teachers in the city system. At the time of our reunion we had 396. The next figures will astound you. In 1942, we had eleven other professional employees in the system and the recent number is eighty-two.

Do you wonder how many people it took to operate the system in '42? Exactly two-a superintendent and a secretary. I hate to ask how many it takes now. With the size of classes back then, it's a wonder we learned to spell our names.

Lots of changes have come about since 1942, but only some have been good. I remember an old song with these words in it: "Fly me to the moon and let me play among the stars." Today we're doing it.

How about the car air-conditioning systems back then? They were the real thing-no artificial stuff. When we wanted air we rolled down the windows and the air rushed in-and I mean rushed in! After every summer date the girls would need another perm.

The process of growing old is the butt of many jokes or expressions. Lists of them are constantly floating around from various sources. I recently found an old list in my filing cabinet with a number of expressions that seem to be on everybody's list. A few of them follow:

1. If they tease you about your age, you can beat them with your cane.

2. It's too late when you know all the answers, because nobody asks you the questions.

3. Over the hill is when the hairline goes back and the waistline goes forward.

4. When you're over the hill everything that doesn't hurt doesn't work.

5. Being over the hill is when your idea of exercise is a good brisk sit.

There's one other thing of note I ran across the other day. It's the Grainger High School annual for the year 1942, the Kay Aitch Ess. Below each of our individual photographs is a caption. Below mine are the descriptive words: Gay, loquacious and witty.

In the same publication there's a page with the heading: <u>Class Prophecy</u>. The editors supposedly prophesied what each student would be dong ten years after graduation. The setting was at an imaginary ball at which former students were present.

I noticed my name was mentioned in the following paragraph: "And Lucy Vaughan, Gordon Heath, Stanley Waldrop, Ellis Aboud, Ray Rouse, Bobby O'Steen and Lawrence Rochelle were just as funny as they are on their comedian programs over the air. They were the life of the party."

Oh, if only that had come true.

Quote of the month from a lady in her 80's who has her share of ailments: "If I had known old age was going to be like this, I would have stayed young."

*　　*　　*

We didn't have an official reunion after our 50th, however, on the 60th anniversary we had an informal get together, and a good crowd gathered at the "Beef Barn". We ate steak and had a grand time chatting and exchanging life stories. That was in 2002.

Sometime after that a small group of men got together and formed what has become known as the "Grainger Men" group. It is not a sanctioned club and there are no dues. We just meet, eat and bring each other up on what's been happening in our lives recently. We usually have as few as ten and as many as eighteen.

Most are domiciled in Kinston, but we have others dropping in from other cities on a rather regular basis. Phil Hines, who lives in Virginia-and who was the driving force behind establishment of the group-comes in regularly form the Norfolk area. Eddie King comes in from Raleigh on a fairly regular basis. Reynolds Carnevale comes in regularly from Fayetteville. Ed Grady comes in regularly from Columbia, SC; others drop in occasionally from out of town.

Even though we are known as the Grainger Men, the name isn't official. Lately it has been mentioned that maybe we should adopt a real name, and a few suggestions have been thrown out for consideration. The one I'm most impressed with was actually suggested by a female. Joyce was in attendance as guest of one of our members, and her entry was ROMEO-"Retired Old Men Eating Out."

Joyce is a main cog in the female version of our group. That group is known as the "Golden Girls" and has been established much longer then ours. Its members are much prettier than ours and they meet weekly, whereas, we meet monthly. Their group is also much more prestigious than ours. And they give such nice gifts on members' birthdays.

Prior to a recent meeting that was held at Joyce's place, the other girls asked if they should bring cards or gifts for Carolyn's birthday. Joyce: "Oh, definitely bring gifts, but I don't know of a thing in the world she needs, except toilet tissue and paper towels."

A couple of days later I was over to Carolyn's. Carolyn: "Ray, if you and Annie should run out of toilet paper, give me a ring."

A Song-Really?

It seems that a number of events have waited until late in my life to occur-some good and others just unusual. This item falls in the category of unusual.

For most of us, I believe, our lives' interests have a tendency to change with the times. As a youngster I was infatuated with Western movies, which at that time we referred to as "Cowboy Shows". As a young adult I was one of the country's most avid baseball fans. At the same time I was a lover of the smooth, soothing music of the Big Band era of the 1940's.

During the 1960's my recreational interest shifted from fishing to golf-and in the 1990's my musical interest was mainly gospel. Annie and I had a routine on Saturday nights of clicking our TV to Lawrence Welk, followed by a gospel hour musical and finally to the Grand Ole Opry. That ended at 11:00, our usual bedtime.

One night during the summer of 1997, one of the "opry" episodes featured that country singer who had lots of black hair that seemed to be piled up high on his head. He was a guitar picker who also wrote country and gospel songs. This fact was emphasized by the emm-cee of the night. At about 10:30 I was enjoying the show and thinking how fortunate some performers were. Not only could they sing and play an instrument, but also had the ability to write music.

While sitting in my recliner, I asked myself, "I wonder if just anybody could write a song?" At that instant a phrase passed through my mind containing these six words: "Will you care for me Lord?"

In response, I immediately left the comfort of my chair and proceeded to the desk in our bedroom. From it I grabbed a ball point and a few sheets of typewriter paper. I sat down and began writing a "song". By bedtime, shortly after 11:00 p.m., I had put on paper what I considered to be one verse and a refrain of a gospel number, which I decided to entitle "Care For Me Lord".

When I woke Sunday about 6:00 a.m., instead of following my usual procedure of going out front to retrieve my morning copy of the Free Press, I grabbed the pen and paper and retreated to one of the tables on the porch. I added a second and third verse to what I had done Saturday night. I still had time to eat, peruse the paper and shower prior to leaving for Sunday school at 9:45.

I had written four stanzas of "something", but so what? They were only words that had descended upon me in a short period of time. Now they needed notes, of which I knew nothing.

*   *   *

It was summer, which meant the choir of Northwest Christian Church was given a two month sabbatical. During that annual interim our music director usually scrounges up what he can to fill the void. One week he asked me if our Sunday school class would pick out a hymn and sing it during church service one Sunday morning.

"I tell you what we'll do, Ned. I've written some words that I believe could become a song. If you will put some notes to them, our class will attempt to sing it to fill one of our Sundays." Done deal.

Bradbury added melody to those words that fitted perfectly. Our group of about fifteen males and females gave forth our rendition of "Care For Me Lord" in the sanctuary of the church on a Sunday morning. With Ned's piano accompaniment, the song was well received by the congregation.

Sometime later I decided to have the thing registered under copyright laws, just for the heck of it. This was one of those "once in a lifetime" events, so I decided to blow twenty bucks by sending the piece to the Library of Congress. It was properly registered and copyrighted in my name.

It had taken several weeks for the process of being registered to be completed, but in due time I received it, properly documented.

Just a few days later I received something else via US Postal Service-correspondence from a recording studio in Hollywood, California. "What is this", I thought, before opening the envelope. It most certainly had to be something pertaining to the song. Could it be that somebody was interested enough in it to make me a financially rewarding offer? This was something new and different.

The envelope contained a form letter that stated the studio's staff had run across "Care For Me Lord" and thought it to be "outstanding". "Boy, this is wonderful", I thought. They had unanimously chosen the song for "screening", a procedure that was needed to answer many questions vital to a successful production. Made sense. This would allow the song to "fit in" with other songs already screened and slated for inclusion in the album our song would be placed in. They were considering the song to be part of an album? Sounded great— —until. There was a catch. The cost of screening would be $333-and was to be borne by Ned and me! Me? This was a little disconcerting. I will admit I knew absolutely nothing about the music publishing business, but I had more or less presumed that if a recording studio wanted to publish a song, it would purchase the right to do so. It would offer a financial incentive to the writer. This did not appear to be happening. That scenario seemed to be reversed in this particular situation.

Their proposed contract did stipulate that if the song should be placed in any commercial, TV show or motion picture by the recording company, we would receive an advance royalty of $2000. But there were some exceptions to even that stipulation.

The contract also stated that if 10,000 albums were sold, they would refund our $333, plus a bonus of $2500. In addition to that, writers of the ten songs on the cassette would receive the sum of

$2.20 for each album sold. That $2.20 would be divided among the writers, which equated to 22 cents each per album.

They also made me a deal on payment of the $333. I could make a down payment of $85, plus four payments of $62 each. I would also be charged a fee of $15 for returned checks. (That really was not a bad fee). Maybe they had checked my financial standing. All this stuff didn't sound too bad upon first reading, but then I began thinking about the 10,000 album sales figures that had to be met in order for anything good too happen to us. It occurred to me that would be a lot of albums to sell, considering the fact all songs would be written by unknowns. I also perused a "please read before signing" warning placed just above the writer signature line. It explained what a high risk venture songwriting was and that only a small percentage of all songs written became "hits". And there was no guarantee the song would earn a profit.

Illusions of grandeur and financial independence began exiting my grey matter. This was simply too much for a failed second grader to absorb, so I decided to ask assistance from an out-of-state relative who, I knew, had some experience along this line. I sent her a copy of everything I had received, including a copy of the song. She was kind enough to make some inquiries which resulted in her relating this message to me, "Don't send any money. If they think the song is good enough to be published, they should be paying you." My sentiments, exactly.

I advised them by mail that I appreciated their gracious consideration of our song, but had decided against signing a contract and forwarding a check.

Not long after receiving above correspondence from that firm, I heard from another recording company which was also domiciled in Hollywood. Its operation and offer were very similar to the other one. Its screening and recording fees were slightly higher than the first one's were, but possible payouts were also greater. I conversed with some of the personnel via telephone who were extremely nice and gave me honest answers to my inquiring questions. Their contract had the same 10,000 sales number. They did, however, guarantee that our song would be in their album soon to be released, in fact, a slot had already been reserved for it. I asked how many albums they had released in the past and found it to be fifteen. Then I asked the vital question: "Of that number, did any of them sell 10,000 copies?" "Frankly, none-we haven't had a hit, yet." I couldn't have asked for a more honest answer. I took the same action on this offer that I did on the first one. Another learning experience late in life-along the path of obtaining a non-university education.

*   *   *

Care For Me Lord

Will you care for me Lord

When I stray from your side,

When I tend to forget who you are?

When I deny you my friend

Will you still remember me,

Though I don't deserve your love?

Will you watch over me

When in times of despair,

Give me strength to return to you Lord?

Keep me in your embrace

And save my wretched soul,

Though I don't deserve your love.

Will you still love me Lord

When I'm not at my best

And not worthy of your precious care?

When I decline to obey

And to Satan give in

And I don't deserve your love.

Refrain:

Yes, care for me Lord.

Please care for me Lord

And enter my heart with love.

Extend your hands, yes give me your hand

And lead me to heaven's door.

This seems to be an appropriate point at which to share with you something which I came across just recently. When I received my "Meals On Wheels" delivery schedule for the month of July, the following bit of humor was typed on the back side:

One day a cat is run over by a car and killed. He ascends into heaven and in short order he is approached by the Lord, who says to the cat, "You lived a good, moral life on earth, for which I want you to be justly rewarded here in heaven. If there is anything special you want in order to make your stay more comfortable here, just let me know."

The cat ponders the statement for a short while and then comes up with this: "Lord, all my life I lived with a poverty-stricken family, and I had to sleep on a hard floor. Most of my fellow cats had soft carpets to help them dream the night away."

"Not to worry" the Lord says. "You shall sleep peacefully from now on." Suddenly, a nice fluffy pillow is lying under the cat's head.

A few weeks afterward, a family of seven mice is killed by an eighteen wheeler. They all go to heaven. Just like with the cat, the Lord soon approaches them and compliments them on the good lives they had lived on earth. He posed the same offer to help that he had earlier made to the cat.

The mice had an immediate request. "Lord, all our lives we have been chased by everything and everybody. We have always had to run from dogs and cats, especially. Men, women and children were constantly trying to hit us with sticks or anything else they could get their hands on. We are tired of running-we want to run no more. What can you do for us?"

"Rest at ease", the Lord says. "I will see that you run no more, I will put you on skates." A few days later the Lord drops by the cat's place and smiles when he sees the cat sleeping peacefully on the soft pillow. The Lord gently stroked his head and asked, "How are things going for you here now?" The cat yawned and stretched his limbs in order to completely awaken. He smiles at the Lord and says, "I'm doing just super. Things couldn't be any better. With this pillow I can sleep all night without batting a wink. And those meals on wheels you've been sending by are the very best."

CHAPTER ELEVEN
LIFE IS—SWINGING ON A STAR

Swinging On A Star

I' ve told you the stories of two most gracious and splendid
ladies. Here is the story of a third, Barbara Creech Rabhan.
A true stalwart.

She is age 86 and makes her residence in a ground floor apartment in a large complex.

When you enter her place you are greeted with an enthusiastic,
"Hello, come in", and a smile. Just a few glances around the apartment
tell you something about this lady. It's as neat as a pin. Everything
is in its place. The beautiful portraits hanging on the walls-painted
by her- give a hint of her artistic ability. And the beautiful Kranich-
Bach piano in her quaint living room, with keys exposed, suggests
other interests as well.

Then my eyes glimpse what appears to be a printed article framed just so-and sitting on a table top just inches away from a framed 8 x 10 picture of our first lady, Laura Bush, properly signed by her.

My eyes are diverted to the framed article. It isn't every day that you walk into a friend's apartment and look upon a letter addressed to the occupant-from the wife of the president of these United States of America. But, there it is, and here it is verbatim:

The White House

August 15, 2001

Ms. Barbara Rabhan

819-F Doctors Drive

Kinston, NC 28501

Dear Ms. Rabhan:

Thank you for your kind and supportive letter and for sending me an inscribed copy of Scrappy's Venture, which I enjoyed and am adding to my library of children's books.

I also enjoy thinking about the hundreds of children you taught in your more than thirty years of teaching. Writer and historian Henry Adams was talking about you when he said that a teacher affects eternity. Your influence on those now-adult children is unending. Thank you for your dedication to teaching.

I am delighted to sign your copy of Scrappy's Venture. I am returning it along with the postage you sent, and a photo I thought you might enjoy.

If I make it to Kinston, I just might take you up on that cup of tea.

With best wishes,

Laura Bush

"On a cold and frosty morning, December 24, 1919, my father and the hired man rode into Kinston, NC, atop a wagon loaded with tobacco. The tobacco was ready for the market at Knott Brothers Warehouse in Kinston.

The tobacco aroma permeated the air. During the fall months and into December, this was a familiar smell in Kinston as the tobacco factories bought and processed the tobacco and shipped it on to Winston-Salem or Durham, NC, to be made into cigarettes, cigars, snuff or chewing tobacco.

Before the hired man drove to the warehouse where he would unload the lot, he dropped my father off at his mother's home.

After greetings and 'How-do's', my father's step-father asked, Where's Eliza? She's home, my father answered.

Take my automobile and go bring her here. You shouldn't have left her there,' he spoke with deep concern.

So my father drove back to Fort Barnwell, Craven County, NC, and brought mother and my brother to Grandmother Ella's home.

One of my aunts said to mother, If you've come to have your baby, you might as well go back. You're not ready to have that baby. The visit moved on as usual; each one telling about family happenings. In due time, everyone was settled down for the night.

About midnight my father was on his way taking mother to Parrott Hospital and just after midnight, early December 24th, I was born. After my first bath I was laid in a dresser drawer made comfortable with swaddling clothes and necessities for a newborn child.

So mother and father were gifted with a Christmas present-'Me'! They were overjoyed. They now had a girl, Barbara, to go along with an older brother, Jay."

I had entered Barbara's apartment to pay a visit and to get a few facts about her life. When I asked her about her birth, what you just read was her written answer.

"Ray, let me go back and tell a bit about my mother's parents. True, they were never famous, but were named for famous ones. Grandmother Barbara was so named from a famous old English ballad, 'Bonnie Barbara Allan.'

Grandfather Emerson was named Thomas Jefferson and was called 'Jeff'. His father was educated for a doctor, but he never practiced-as he preferred lecturing to an audience.

Grandfather Emerson dressed up in white starched and ironed shirt, hooked the buggy to 'Old Gatsy' and rode off for the day, leaving the work to the others. That was his daily routine.

Grandmother Barbara took responsibilities seriously. I remember seeing her let the butter in a pail down in the deep well to keep it cool in summer. She would prepare her food on Saturday for Sunday, and keep it in the deep well, also.

Grandmother Barbara married her step-brother."

"Barbara, can you tell me anything about yourself as a child?"

"Well, we lived at Fort Barnwell in Craven County when I was born, but I remember so little about it, because we moved back to Greene County while I was still a small child. I do remember, though, an elderly couple named Tilghman. Mr. Tilghman wore a long bushy beard. Mrs. Tilghman wore a draw string cap and a long white apron as one might have been wearing in the kitchen of the Tryon Palace. I remember going over to their home when we were invited there for a hot cup of coffee and cookies-and steaming hot chocolate for the children.

Mother said we had a front porch that was high off the ground-and that I would crawl across the porch, carefully get my legs to the edge and enjoy swinging my little legs back and forth and enjoy the fresh air on a sunny day. Neighbors told mother they were afraid I would fall off the porch, but I never did.

When I was still a small child we moved away from Fort Barnwell and went back to Greene County to a farm my granddaddy owned. A few years later my father bought his own farm in the same neighborhood.

My granddaddy was John Creech, who died at about age 28 of pneumonia.

I also remember at pre-school age a cyclone hit our property and one of the big barns was damaged, but no one was hurt.

And then there was the time a rabid dog found his way into our neighborhood and we were warned not to stray from the house.

But the thing I remember most about my very young childhood involved the loss of my favorite doll, Polly."

"Can you tell me what exactly happened?"

"I can do better than that. I wrote a poem about the incident some years ago, and called it 'Polly's Fate.' Here it is, read it."

Polly's Fate
This is a real-life's story
I always will remember.
More than 80 years ago
In the month of September.

It happened to be in haying time.
The workers gathered it in.
Winter's food for the horses,
They stored it in the bin.

The sweet aroma of the hay
To both horses and to me.
As I stood in the barnyard door
Where I could smell and see.

In my arms I held my doll.
Polly was her name.
Her head was empty as could be,
But I loved her just the same.

She was not made of China

Nor cloth doll was she.

She was fashioned in a mould.

Santa brought her to me.

Polly was my companion.

She didn't have a brain.

She never ever frowned at me,

Nor did she complain.

In the barnyard door I was standing

With Polly in my arm.

Never ever had a thought

Of destiny or of harm.

When up came old Gatsy,

The biggest of the lot.

He snapped off my dolly's head,

Left me a crying tot!

"That's how it happened. If you're wondering what happened to the doll's head after it was severed, Ray, Gatsy ate it-the whole thing. I recall the doll being made of some kind of construction paper and he must have thought it was hay.

I entered first grade at Hookerton High School when I was five years old. We rode a school bus, a trip of possibly seven or eight miles. I was not a top notch student but I graduated on time in 1936. I really believe I was not ready for school at age five, but I didn't fail any grades.

I took piano lessons when I was in the third grade. That was when I fell in love with music. I progressed so fast that in the fourth grade at commencement exercises at Hookerton School I played Dvorak's Humoresque, a classical piece. In the sixth grade I played for Rainbow Methodist Church. Actually, the church had burned down and the congregation was meeting in a farm barn owned by Frank Jones. The organ was one of those pump types. While in the sixth grade I was also asked to play for the high school assembly.

In the fourth grade my interest in art appeared when I drew a picture of a cardinal with a yellow beak, a red crest and black markings. It was so pretty the teacher passed it around for the students to see. Somehow, the drawing never got back to me. I remember when I was in the fifth grade I hid construction paper in my desk and I would get it out and draw when I was supposed to be doing other studies."

"Barbara, can you remember any other interesting events you might have had in your early life?"

"Yes, I do. Sometime before I entered school I had a serious thing happen to me. We heated our house with a big old fireplace. Several logs were placed in the fireplace and fire was started by putting a lightwood splinter under the logs after setting it on fire with a match. I did this once without my parent's knowledge-a near catastrophe! I allowed the burning splinter to get too close to my pajamas and they caught fire. Mother grabbed a blanket quickly and wrapped it around me, extinguishing the flame, but not before I suffered some burns which left scars on my abdominal area. I don't believe I was taken to a doctor. My parents treated me at home."

"Barbara, you know you and I are kin somewhere down the line. Just how does that come about?"

"My mother, who died in 1984, was named Eliza Emerson Creech. My father, who died in 1961, was Jesse Wyatt Creech. I understand your mother, Lillie Creech, was my father's first cousin. I believe that makes us third cousins."

"Ok 'cuz'-I know you didn't get your education 'out behind the barn'-so where did you go to college?"

"I attended East Carolina Teacher's College in Greenville. It was referred to then as ECTC. It's now East Carolina University. I believe its original name was East Carolina Training College.

My major was primary education, but I also pursued my musical and art interests. Both would prove valuable to me later as a school teacher.

My first job was teaching sixth grade in a school at Winterville, a small place just three or four miles south of Greenville. I stayed there four years. I later taught at Lewis, Harvey and Northwest schools in Kinston."

"How about your love life, Barbara? When did you start dating?"

"Well, Mother encouraged me along that line. She had a horror of me becoming an old maid. I first dated at age 19-a blind date with a boy named Carroll Oakes. That was the only time we dated each other. I dated a number of boys while at ECTC, but I didn't get serious with any of them until one night I met THE boy on a blind date."

"Why was this particular boy appealing to you?"

"First of all, he was good looking, blue eyes, black hair, and good physique. He had lovely manners and was witty. What girl would not have been attracted to him? He was also organized, a trait seldom seen in boys that age, and he exhibited ambition. In addition, he had finished junior college. He was a year younger than I. He had a purple car that we named 'Deep Purple', after the song.

I still dated other boys, but Jim turned out to be the special one. Not only that-my parents knew his father (his mother was deceased) and they wholeheartedly approved of my dating him. Mother was delighted, foreseeing a marriage sometime in the future. My father even bought a farm, which he promised to give me at the time of our marriage.

Jim, however, had other plans for his near future. He and my brother decided to volunteer for military service. I believe that was in 1940, prior to the war. He became a bombardier in the U.S. Army Air Corps, and was stationed in the Pacific area.

All these future plans were being made by my family, but he and I had actually dated only a relatively few times before he joined the army. And the dating game in those days was totally different from that of today.

Even though Mother had always encouraged me to go out with the opposite sex, she was a prude, and she constantly reminded me what not to do on dates. And I had always made a practice of obeying my parents.

The first boy who kissed me simply pecked me on the cheek. A short time later he wrote me a note telling me how much he enjoyed the kiss. Somehow, Mother got hold of that note and she gave me down the country. She let me know in no uncertain terms that it was not to happen again.

Only one time did Jim kiss me. It happened one night as he was leaving our house after spending a short time with me. During that visit we were never out of sight of one of my parents until Jim reached the front door to leave. The door had four large glass panels and one was broken out. He had opened the door and stepped onto the porch. As the door closed, I stuck my head out the broken panel to say good night. When I did, he bent down and kissed my cheek. That was our first and last kiss. I was a college sophomore then.

I dated others, including servicemen, after he entered the military, but we corresponded on a fairly regular basis."

*　　*　　*

On December 7, 1941, the world changed for all Americans. The nations of Europe had been at war since 1939, when the axis powers of Germany, Italy, and Japan took on the remaining countries in an attempt to gain control of the world. When Japanese planes bombed Pearl Harbor on that fateful day in December, it became truly a world war in every respect. World War II became the greatest war in the history of mankind and it didn't end until August 1945.

Not long after war was declared by President Franklin D. Roosevelt, correspondence with Jim ceased. Friends and family wondered and worried.

Soon after war was declared families began receiving telegrams from the US Government notifying them of the death, missing in action, or imprisonment of their loved ones.

Nothing was heard about Jim for months, but eventually his dad received a message from the Adjutant-General's office in Washington, D.C. It advised the father that heavy casualties had been inflicted by the enemy at the Battle of Corregidor, where Jim reportedly last saw action. It was also stated that it was possible his son was killed or taken prisoner. It was not good news to the father, nor to Barbara.

The next communication which came from the government stated that the son was, in fact, being held by the Japanese as a prisoner of war on Taiwan Island. Afterwards, sporadic messages were received by the father from his son. It wasn't unusual for the son to ask his dad to say hello to Barbara for him.

By this time Barbara had graduated from ECTC and was teaching at a school in Winterville. Life went on for her. She dated US Marines quite frequently who were stationed at Camp Lejeune, only about fifty miles from Kinston. It was 1945 and it had been quite a long while since hearing anything from Jim. Her mother encouraged her to pursue other romantic interests, since it was possible she would never see Jim again.

Barbara had a routine of going home to Greene County on weekends. Since gasoline was rationed during the war, she usually caught the bus that ran from Greenville to Kinston-and made stops in Winterville.

On this particular day she entered the bus and paid the fee and sat down beside a male passenger. At some point the passenger exited the bus before it reached Kinston. When that happened, another passenger moved out of the seat he had been occupying and moved to where Barbara was sitting.

"Do you mind if I sit here beside you?" "No, not at all."

Isn't it strange how casual meetings can change the course of life for many of us? On those occasions that big little word, "If", comes into prominence.

When that young man sat down beside Barbara something magical seemed to occur inside him. He was awestruck and he apparently fell in love with her right there on the bus. His manners were impeccable and he made an immediate impression upon her. That same feeling did not overwhelm her, but in her own words, he more or less swept her off her feet. When he arrived at his Kinston destination he reportedly told one of the Brody brothers that he had just met the woman he was going to marry.

That was in the spring of 1945. It had been an extended period of time since she had heard from Jim. Was he still a prisoner of war? Had he died from POW hardship? Her mother had been suggesting she get serious with someone, because she might never see Jim again. She was vulnerable and very much prey. Here was a man who had made a great impression on her and she knew he was totally in love with her. It seemed a perfect scenario for marital matchup.

And it occurred. Thoughts of Jim seemingly left her and a wedding was agreed upon. The ceremony was performed within a short time on July 14, 1945. Her mother needn't worry any longer about her becoming an old maid.

Morton and Barbara Rabhan moved into an apartment in Greenville, NC. He was now living in the city of his employment and her teaching position in Winterville was not much more than a stone's throw away. They were settling down into a life of marriage.

Just one month later she would receive the shock of her young life.

"I was at home from work one day when the doorbell rang. When I opened the door there stood a delivery boy from a local florist. I thought-who would be sending me flowers, or was it one of those wrong address situations? The young man confirmed the address and told me the dozen red roses were from "Jim". What a shock! I can't describe exactly how I felt. Consternation-certainly. Dismay-probably. Happiness-in no way. Elated-just the opposite.

THE boy, the one I had that special feeling for five or six years ago, was safely home. No more a prisoner of war. And he had sent me roses! What could I do? Nothing. Absolutely nothing! I was already married. I had been for a month. There was nothing I could do. I gave the roses back to the delivery boy and instructed him to deliver them to Jim's sister's address with my regards.

When Morton came home from work I told him what had happened. He told me he would not have objected to my keeping the roses."

IF that chance meeting on that bus had not occurred in the little village of Winterville, NC in the spring of 1945, what would have been the course of Barbara Creech's life?

Whatever might have happened didn't really matter. Morton Rabhan put Barbara on a pedestal and adored her until his death of congestive heart failure in March, 1984 at age 69.

Morton was thought to be a Jew by many people, but he was not. His parents were but he was not. He never attended a synagogue the entire time Barbara knew him. He attended church with her at a Disciples of Christ church wherever they lived. They produced two children. Samuel lives in Goldsboro, NC and Sandra Kaye in Greensboro, NC.

"Barbara, how did your two families react to the marriage? Was there joy, disappointment, or what? After all, you say your mother had always been afraid of the old maid thing for you. Now that you had a husband who was presumably Jewish, how did she feel about your being a wife? After all, Jew-Gentile marriages were rather uncommon events in that day and time."

"I can tell you Ray, Morton's family embraced me immediately. They were overjoyed and treated me like a daughter from the beginning.

As for my family, they were apprehensive at first. They assumed him to be a Jew, since his parents were Jewish. Mother told me she was afraid I might lose some of my friends because I had married a Jew.

Their attitude changed, though, when they realized how deeply Morton was in love with me-and they came to know him as the fine person he was. In time, mother developed deep love for Morton-and during the last three years of her life she lived with Morton and me."

*   *   *

"Barbara, what happened to Jim, did you ever see him after the rose bouquet event?"

"Yes. Our two families were friends and it wasn't too unusual for both of us to appear at the same neighborhood gettogether. Our relationship on those occasions was cordial. Not long after returning home he went to Florida and married and remained there. His wife died not too long ago and he came by to pay me a visit while he was in Kinston.

We reminisced and talked about each other's family and what we had done in life since we last saw each other. We have corresponded once since he returned to Florida."

* * *

In 1959 the family moved to the area of High Point, NC. They actually lived in Jamestown, which was a suburb of High Point. The house they bought there was located on Guilford County Road-on property which had been owned by the Mackay family as a farm. It had been known as a great place to quail hunt and many hunters visited it for that purpose. In fact, Irving Berlin, the great songwriter who wrote more than 900 songs, made expeditions to the farm to hunt the birds. He also took a fancy to the farm owner's daughter-which resulted in his taking a Tar Heel for a wife.

While living there Barbara exercised an opportunity to purchase 30 acres of the land from Mittie Wilson, a friend and substitute school teacher. She grew hay on the property for about four years and then sold the entire acreage for a very handsome profit. The new owners developed it into a high rise apartment complex.

It was in High Point where Morton entered the furniture manu-facturing business, but after a few years he went out of business and became a representative for a number of manufacturers. They remained in High Point for about twenty years.

While there she taught school and attended art classes at night. She also used her expertise to write plays and songs for students to present in school activities.

Prior to 1998 she enjoyed taking extensive trips to such places as Canada, Haiti, Alaska, several islands, Australia, and New Zealand. She also enjoyed cruises and she took a number of them. On the cruise to Alaska she met an old man with whom she danced a number of times. He called her Margaret Thatcher and wanted her to marry him. After returning from her trip he visited her twice at her home in an attempt to get her to say, 'Yes', but she turned him down. She also enjoyed a trip to Nova Scotia with her sister in 1986 where they witnessed the tide at the Bay of Fundy.

I mention the year 1998 because that was a pivotal year in the life of Barbara Creech Rabhan. It was a year in which her whole life was turned upside down. Nothing would ever be the same after that year.

It was during a routine physical by her physician that a debacle manifested itself. She had been feeling good and had no idea there was anything wrong with her physically. Dr. Jilcott found otherwise. He noticed what appeared to be an uncontrolled movement in one of her limbs. She hadn't even been aware of it. He made a diagnosis almost immediately. He told her she had a unique disease that was similar to Parkinson's-but it was not Parkinson's disease. It was Essential Benign Tremors. She got the same diagnosis from a total of seven doctors. It's so rare that hers is the only case Dr. Jilcott has ever treated.

Many people in our world suffer from tremors. This simply means that a person does not have control of one or more movements of either hands, head, limbs, or voice. Sometimes this occurs as a reaction to circumstances such as fear or anger. When tremors occur without any apparent cause, then they can be a sign of essential tremors which, like Parkinson's, is a neurological disorder. This illness is referred to as the Katherine Hepburn disease, since she purportedly suffered from it in her latter years. It apparently will not kill you, however, because she lived to be age 96.

Previously in that same year of 1998, Barbara had suffered her first catastrophe, the loss of sight in her right eye due to cataract surgery.

It was during her recovery from that disaster that she wrote, illustrated, and published her book, "Scrappy's Venture".

It's a wonderful book for children that depicts the life of a mother raccoon and her five babies: Whacky, Scaky, Flossie, Flea, and Scrappy-the mischievous one. The story has a moral: children, obey your parents.

*　　　*　　　*

"Barbara, what do you miss mostly by having this tremors disability?"

"Well, first of all, I was amazed at the rapidity in which it evolved. As you know, I wasn't even aware I had it when I walked in Dr. Jilcott's office that day, but just six months later I was in such bad shape that I knew I shouldn't drive, so I gave up my car. You can imagine how much I missed that.

And my love for painting has always been in my life. When my arms and hands became so shaky I could no longer hold a brush, it was a blow."

"But, Barbara, how is it you can still play a piano?"

"As you can see, my entire body shakes, but when I touch things with my limbs the shaking stops. For instance, when I take a glass in my hand, it stops shaking and I can drink without spilling its contents. The same thing applies to my hands. When my fingers touch the keys they stop shaking. Isn't it wonderful that I can still play?

I also miss the social life I once had. I always enjoyed the extended trips and cruises I was fortunate enough to be able to take. I'm so glad I had that opportunity to see so much of the world after returning to Kinston after spending 20 years in High Point.

I've heard people say, 'you can't go back home', but you can. I renewed old friendships and just had a wonderful time here. I have fond memories of one trip especially.

It occurred in the 1980's when I was a North Carolina Symphony Board Member. One year the board put on a contest to see who could sell the most tickets for the coming season. Lo and behold, I was the winner. The prize was a ticket for two for a one week trip to anywhere in the United States.

My friend, Hettie Whitaker, suggested I go to the Seattle area-and she would be glad to escort me-inasmuch as her sister lived in Spokane. And she would be glad to put us up for the week. Done deal. That's exactly what we did. I recall taking a boat ride while there, as well as traveling to Boise, Idaho, on a sightseeing trip.

Another thing I surely miss are the worship services at Gordon Street Christian Church. My uncontrollable guttural sounds would be distracting."

* * *

She also bursts out with uncontrollable laughter at times and she has trouble talking coherently. She has to stop at times to search for words. And she has trouble holding a book in order to read.

When she purchased a copy of my "They Didn't Bring Ice on Sunday", she didn't think she could hold it up long enough to read. I made arrangements to read it to her while she lay in bed. That seems to be the position she's most comfortable in. I believe she enjoyed every word. I would laugh with her and I would cry with her. It makes you feel good when you can make someone else feel good simply by reading to them.

It's very possible that Barbara inherited the illness she has. She says her father became shaky before he died. Her father's mother also possessed a trait of shakiness. In addition, a first cousin's nephew suffered from the Lou Gehrig disease.

Even though I had never heard of Essential Benign Tremors prior to Barbara's case, I understand ordinary tremors are more common than Parkinson's. It's more common in the elderly. But it isn't too unusual for a young person to come down with it.

"Barbara, I know how this malady has affected you physically, but how about your eating habit. Has that changed in any way?"

"I should say it has. I've become like a caterpillar. I want to eat all the time. When I finish breakfast, I'm ready for lunch. When I finish lunch, I'm ready for dinner."

"What's your favorite food?"

"I guess my very favorite thing is a dessert-lemon chess pie-but I also love that good old southern fried chicken. I don't eat beef and I don't drink milk."

"You must have taken after my mother. She didn't drink nor eat any dairy product. It seems that before I was born she came down with tuberculosis. Her treatment consisted of living on the back porch and drinking milk and eating ice cream for several months. She became so saturated with dairy products that when she recuperated, she chose not to indulge in them for the remainder of her life.

Yes, Lillie Creech Rouse became a picky eater and it rubbed off on me, her son.

My curiosity has got the best of me, Barbara; did your dad ever give you that farm he planned to give you if you married Jim?"

"Actually, he did. It was sometime in the 1950's. And I still own it."

"How about your favorite song? I know you have one."

"Of course, and it's that hymn that John Newton wrote so many years ago-'Amazing Grace'. What a wonderful song with such a wonderful message. I've played it so many times over the years."

"I'll bet you have a favorite scripture, also, don't you?"

"Yes, and it has such a promise in it: 'Seek ye first the Kingdom of God and his righteousness and all these things shall be added unto you.'"

"Looking back on your life, Barbara, with the misfortunes you've had, do you hold any bitterness toward anyone?"

"No, Ray, not toward anyone. I've lost the sight of an eye and have contracted this terrible disease, but I have so much to be thankful for.

First of all, I have two beautiful Christian children to be thankful for. And even with my infirmities I still have a good mind. I can walk, I can talk, I can see. I can hear without an aide. I can smell. I thank God for all these things I still possess.

I'm thankful for friends who stop by so often to share some time with me. I'm thankful for the help I get several hours daily by the nicest young lady. I'm fortunate to have such a person as a caregiver."

"Do you fear death?"

"No, I don't fear death at all. You see, I have that peace that passes all understanding. I have reached that point in life where I have achieved total contentment.

I've been thinking about-maybe this disability has been a blessing in disguise. This confinement has brought me closer to God. It has enabled me to concentrate on Him rather than on the worldly things of life.

I thank God daily for blessing me all these years, and I don't have a problem forgiving anybody who has transgressed against me. I am happier today than at any other time in my life."

"Barbara, this has been nice, but I have to go. But before I do, how about pulling that stool up to the baby grand and let me hear you tickle those keys?"

No sooner said than done. When she placed her fingers on those keys, it was just like magic. The trembling in her hands seemed to stop and her fingers became nimble. She played from memory one of those great songs from the Big Band era, "Swinging on a Star." She didn't miss a note. She was enjoying it as much as I. What a great way to part!

As I left, two thoughts ran through my mind: "What wonders God has wrought" and "there, but for the grace of God, go I."

May God continue to bless you, Barbara Creech Rabhan.

*   *   *

We live in an imperfect world, an imperfect nation, an imperfect state, and an imperfect locale-among imperfect people. If we cannot adapt to this fact and get on with our lives, we might never be the recipient of a life of true contentment that Barbara Rabhan possesses.

CHAPTER TWELVE
LIFE IS — GOOD

W hen I say life is good, there will be many who will disagree
with that statement, and rightly so. There are periods in
the lives of all of us when we question the validity of the remark.

I think of my own parents. Pop was an easy-going fellow who
appeared to worry very little, if at all. He lost his farm in 1918 when
a severe hailstorm hit his tobacco crop and he was unable to meet his
financial commitments that fall.

From that time on, during the Great Depression, jobs were on a
hit and miss basis until he was finally able to secure one as fertil-
izer salesman, which he remained on until old age. He was one of
those people who loved life in good times and bad times. In his latter
years he was happy as long as he could get a good cigar or a chew
of tobacco-and collard greens.

Up until age 89 he had no sickness except for a hemorrhoidectomy at age 65. No more problems until age 89. At that time a bunion on his big toe ruptured and blood poison entered his leg. He was given a choice between amputation and death. Having enjoyed life for 89 years, he wanted more of it. "Take the leg." He recovered and entered a nursing home without complaint and resumed the good life. Not long after he entered the facility he died instantly after indulging in a good breakfast. He had asked the nurse to get him his plug of chewing tobacco-and he died before she could give it to him. He still had good mental ability, just three weeks before he would have reached his 90th birthday. Life had been good to him for his entire tenure on earth and he enjoyed it to the last breath.

With Mama it was a different story. She was in poor health ever since I can remember. She had suffered through a period of tuberculosis before I was born. I recall her being on blood pressure diets and medicines for many years. She also claimed to have heart trouble. She was little, but tough, and a hard worker. She more or less handled the family's finances, if you could call it that. At any rate, Pop handed over his paycheck to her and she paid the bills. She was a worrier and got very little pleasure out of life. She was the exact opposite of Pop. Work and worry took their toll on her. At one point in her late seventies I recall her having a short spell of hallucinations. She imagined bugs being in the house and on clothes in the closets. Each of us children searched and searched the apartment and never could see any evidence of any kind of bug. At someone's suggestion we engaged a local exterminating firm to go to the apartment and do some spraying. We told Mama this was going to happen and she would need to stay somewhere else while the spraying was being done. Within a few hours we brought her back and advised her that the bugs had been done away with, even though the exterminator had also failed to find any signs of bugs. That completely satisfied her and no mention of insects was made afterwards.

Her health gradually deteriorated and she became confined to a nursing home. She wasn't too happy there and she finally broke a hip and had mini-strokes. She died at age 86. Two or three years before she died she began saying she wanted to die. She said there was nothing else she wanted out of life. Her mentality deteriorated and before she passed away she couldn't call my name correctly. In many ways life had not been too good for her.

Then I think of my brother, Biggie, who lives with his wife, Christine. He is now 88 and she is one year older than he. He is a person who had thrived on hard work and made a living doing it-and he enjoyed life.

He retired in his early sixties and has enjoyed every minute of his no-work period. Until just a few years ago he spent a great deal of his retirement fresh water fishing, which you might say was the recreation love of his life. When he could get to a river or creek and slowly motor to his favorite fishing spot and drop a line into the water with a cricket at the end of it, that was heaven on earth to him. He didn't want to take much time eating or drinking, he just wanted to see that cork go under. About eight years ago he suffered a stroke that set him back physically, but he can still drive to church and the supermarket. He also cooks and prepares meals for his wife, Christine, and himself. She uses a "scooter" to get around the house. Biggie still has his mental faculties, even though he admits he's not as sharp as he once was. I've referred to him at times as a human calculator. He could run figures through his head as fast as some people can use an adding machine. All with a tenth grade education. He considers himself one of the luckiest people around and will tell you how good life has been to him. I've heard him say more than once that life owes him nothing.

Christine comes from a line of long livers. She had one sister to die a couple of years ago at age 100 and she has a sister living who, I believe, is 90, or over. Even being partially disabled with arthritis, she also says life has been very good to her, especially during her years of retirement. She is age 89.

On the other hand, Annie had an aunt who was the first person I ever heard of being diagnosed with Alzheimer's disease. When I first heard of it I couldn't spell the word nor pronounce it. It was described as a pulling away of the brain from the skull and was a disease for which there was no cure. I believe onset of the sickness was in her middle age and it lasted for nineteen years. Her case was a worst scenario situation in which she had to be watched every minute to keep her from such actions as putting her hand on a hot stove. Her husband died before she did, leaving care for her up to her children. She was in a nursing home for a while, but by and large she was kept at home and taken care of by her loving children until she passed away. I couldn't honestly say life was good to her.

———————

It's amazing to me how many people will say life has been good to them, even though they have suffered with a debilitating disease.

I'm thinking of Lou Gehrig, one of the greatest baseball players of all time, who played in the Babe Ruth era of the 1930's. In fact, he played alongside Ruth and many fans consider him the best first baseman of all time. In addition to being a great glove player, he was also a great batter. He and Ruth batted back to back for years and they became the most feared twosome in baseball in that period.

He joined the New York Yankees on June 11, 1923 as a tremendously well built person with a shy attitude. He was a very conservative spender, not buying his first automobile until 1927, when he bought a used Packard at a cost of $700. This, despite the fact he had the income of a major league baseball player.

He was an immediate success and in 1928 he was rated the fourth most popular athlete in the country behind Jack Dempsey, Babe Ruth, and Gene Tunney.

Even though he was both a great fielder and hitter, he is most remembered for setting an endurance record by playing in the most consecutive games of any major leaguer.

That wasn't easy and at times he resorted to extraordinary means to accomplish the feat. At one time he played with a cast on his thumb.

On another occasion he was so ill that he couldn't dress himself. In order to keep his streak going his manager dressed him and took him to the dugout. The game's lineup was changed, putting Gehrig in the leadoff spot. Players escorted him to the batter's box to become the first batter of the game. After his turn at bat he was taken out of the game without ever going to his fielding position. As long as he made any appearance in a game, it was counted as official and kept his streak alive. His streak was prolonged a number of times by rainouts.

His narrowest escape occurred in 1934. It was during an exhibition game during the season against the Norfolk Tars, a Yankee farm team which played in the Piedmont League. The game was played in Norfolk. The pitcher for the Tars was a guy named Ray White. It was known that he and Gehrig didn't like each other from an earlier incident.

A fast ball, high and inside, hit Lou in his forehead-about two inches above his right eye. He hit the ground-out cold. He didn't make a move. Nothing but quietness in the stadium. He was revived and taken to a hospital for x-rays. They showed no fracture, just a brain concussion which happened occasionally to ball players. The streak would surely be broken the next day.

Wrong! He played the next day and hit three triples in three at-bats. The welt on his head was so big he couldn't wear his own cap, so he borrowed one from Babe Ruth and let it out to the maximum so it would fit over Lou's knot.

A short time after the incident White made this remark, "I didn't throw at him, but somebody had to stop that streak!"

In 1938 Lou Gehrig, the great physical specimen with thighs that looked as big as hams, was first struck with Amyotrophic Lateral Sclerosis (ALS), that horrible rare disease from which nobody had ever known to survive. Nevertheless, he was still able to play in the 1938 season but his game deteriorated badly. On September 27, 1938 he hit his last home run, the 493rd of his career. The last game he played was on April 30, 1939. His record streak had ended at 2130.

On July 4, 1939, the Lou Gehrig Appreciation Day was held between double header games at Yankee Stadium. Sixty thousand fans were on hand to pay honors to an unassuming young man who had meant so much to the game of baseball-and had been a role model to so many youngsters. I was a fifteen-year- old and an avid baseball fan. I never missed a game at the local ballpark. The old Coastal Plain League was where many future major league stars began their career, one of which was Charlie Keller.

I kept abreast of major league action and I recall the day Lou Gehrig made his famous remarks while standing on home plate at Yankee Stadium on that July day.

He was a shy person who usually tried to stay in the background, never a "hot dog", like so many present day athletes.

He really didn't want to go through this day which had been set aside especially for him. He made the remark that he would give a month's pay in order to get out of the proceedings.

At much urging of his manager and the club's owner, he finally stepped out very timidly from the dugout and walked, with help, toward home plate where microphones were. It was a distance of about ten yards. His head was hung the entire time.

After a number of introductions and speeches were made extolling him as one of the greatest players of all time and a true gentleman, the crowd began to yell, "We want Lou!"

When he moved to home plate and wiped his eyes again, the crowd of 60,000 people became totally silent. Not a sound of any kind. It was as if the earth had stopped turning. One fan described later how he had felt at that moment by saying, "I felt chills up and down my spine." I know what that feeling must have been. I felt the same sensation many times while in the army during World War II when our entire battalion assembled on parade grounds at the end of a day. When the huge Army band played the "Star Spangled Banner" while we stood at attention, I felt shivers run up and down my back. You could call it patriotism, or whatever, but in those moments I felt proud to a part of an organization training to take part in saving the world from tyrants.

Seconds seemed like eons. No one spoke. Finally, Lou bent over toward the microphones, took a deep breath and began speaking.

"For the past two weeks, you've been reading about a bad break. Today, I consider myself the luckiest man on the face of the earth." After speaking those immortal words, he continued by paying homage to the baseball people around him who had helped his career, to the groundskeepers, sports writers, his parents, and his wife. He then finished with these words, "So, I close in saying that I might have had a bad break, but I have an awful lot to live for."

Yes, Lou Gehrig was truly a good man who had lived a good life.

A Capitol Fourth

There are times in life when some of us need to make a fresh start-turn things around-try to make things better. This can happen to groups, corporations or individuals.

A few nights ago, July 4th, I was watching the PBS show: "A Capitol Fourth". The M.C. introduced one of the performers whose name was Ronan Tynan, and briefly mentioned a few details of his life. He told how Tynan had made a fresh start at a young age and had became extremely successful in his attempt to secure a good life.

He is a native of Ireland who, at age 20, had both legs amputated due to serious injuries sustained in an auto accident. He was a student at the time and had such determination that within weeks he was able to climb the stairs of his college dormitory. During that same year he participated in the Paralympics and won a number of gold medals.

He pursued a medical degree, but at age 33-when he was well into his residency-he decided to take formal voice study and within one year's time, he won twice in voice competitions. He eventually became one of the three Irish Tenors, and helped the group become sensational world wide.

He works as a single now and sings many types of music. He sang at President Reagan's Funeral and performed a number of times after the Twin Towers debacle in New York. He participated in memorial services for members whose lives were lost in the tragedy.

He did a tremendous job singing "God Bless America" in the Capitol Fourth concert, a song which he has sung a number of times at Yankee Stadium. He now calls New York his home away from home. A great success story for one who made a new start and was extremely successful in attaining that good life for himself.

Thanksgiving

And how about the Pilgrims? That group of 110 people made the decision of their lives when they decided to go to a new country thousands of miles away to seek a better life.

The group had left England in 1609 and migrated to Holland to live in an environment where religious freedom prevailed. They seemed to prosper there, but for whatever reason, they became dissatisfied and decided they wanted to go to the New World they had heard about, in order to make a completely new life. They wanted a new start and a good life.

On September 6, 1620 the group set sail on the Mayflower from Plymouth, England, on a sojourn that would severely test their patience and fortitude. Sixty-five days later, after suffering illness and hardship, the shores of the New World were sighted.

After landing at a place now known as Plymouth, Massachusetts, they suffered through a winter so harsh that only about 50 souls survived. They persevered, however, and with help from native Indians they managed to survive.

During their third year, November 29th was declared a time set aside for giving thanks to the Lord for the prosperity they had achieved. That incident, of course, evolved into our present Thanksgiving Day. That group of people had succeeded in their venture to obtain a good life.

Just what is a good life? We hear the expression spoken quite frequently. At funerals, especially. It isn't unusual to hear an attendant speak of the deceased as having lived a good life. Specifically, exactly what would he be referring to? Would he mean the person had lived a life of high moral values and was a law abider? Did he mean the person had been a good provider for his family and had always been faithful to his wife? Did he mean the deceased had been a philanthropist and had spent his life helping others? Or was he referring to just an ordinary person who made a habit of helping ordinary people whose lives were made better by his gracious actions?

If this is what the attendant was thinking of, all of us know people who would fit in that category.

I knew such a person who died just last year, a friend of many years-Hazel Davis. She succumbed after suffering about three years with cancer. She had spent her life constantly doing things to help people in time of need. This was her way of showing love and compassion for others. In many cases she was the first person to hear of a need-and she responded. She had a nice habit of taking food to the bereaved or flowers to the sick. She was generous to poor families who needed help. She was a tireless worker for her church.

At her memorial service at Northwest Christian Church, her son-in-law asked for people in attendance to raise their hands if Hazel had ever helped them in any way. Almost every hand in the full sanctuary was raised. Yes, Hazel Davis lived the good life.

Professionals

Thankfully, there are many in the medical field of this country who reach out beyond their normal field of practice and donate their time and expertise to help others. There are many people who, due to no fault of their own, are unable to help themselves. One of their great needs is dental care, which is not usually covered by entitlement programs. This need is being met here in our City of Kinston.

It must have been about 1959 when I first met Dr. Junius Rose, Jr., who would soon become known as "June" to everyone.

He and his wife, Sarah, moved on Parrott Avenue, just around the corner from our place on West Road. Their son, Skippy, was about five years old and our son, Mike, was four. The two of them would later become members of the neighborhood bunch. Their daughter, Elizabeth, was probably about a year old. Our daughter, Cindy, was an infant.

I must have been age 35 at that time-and I had not occupied a chair in a dentist's office since age 18, when I had two teeth pulled. It seemed the army dentists didn't want to spend the time it took to fill a tooth. If a cavity existed, it was simpler and quicker just to pull it. Inasmuch as I was ignorant of the whole dental bit, I voiced no objection. As scarce as money was in our household when I was a kid, food and clothing were more important than dental care, so my Fort Bragg dental experience was my first one. I had brushed my teeth regularly and was not aware of a cavity until I was drafted. All those sweet rolls and Pepsi I drank as a kid must have taken a toll.

After my military discharge in 1945 I did not change my dental habit. I continued to brush, but nothing more. Soon after Dr. Rose moved into the neighborhood I decided maybe I should have a dental checkup-and who would be better than June Rose? I became his patient and I saw him with some irregularity at first and finally on a regular basis. I have one crown in my mouth, which he provided me with years ago, and it's still there. I recall him apologizing to me for the cost, which I believe was seventy dollars.

At some point in time he told me if I would obey his instructions, he would get me into my seventies with the teeth I had. I am close to 82 and I have all those teeth except one.

Dr. Rose sold his practice in 1997, but he left me in the good hands of Dr. Scott Matthews, a gem of a little fellow who seems to be following in June's footsteps.

I think June actually retired for about a year, but then decided he wasn't ready for full retirement. What he really wanted to do was to help people who were not able to afford normal dental care, especially children.

That want of his to help others goes back a long way. It might have had its beginning when, fresh out of dental school, he agreed to a stint of twelve months at the Dorothea Dix Institution, but wound up staying there for twenty-seven months. Later in his career he would do other charitable work.

That desire of his was satisfied when he was able to secure a small room in the Kinston Community Health Center building. There he could set up a dental chair where he could begin giving dental care to those who could never afford it. Two chairs have now multiplied to twelve and there are four full-time dentists in the clinic.

In November of 2005 the community showed its appreciation to Dr. Rose for all he had done for the underprivileged of this area. At that time about 300 people congregated at a gathering sponsored by the Lenoir County Chapter of the American Red Cross, at which Dr. Rose was named the first recipient of the Kinstonian of the Year award. The designation couldn't have been bestowed to a more deserving person.

Dr. Junius Rose, Jr., has lived a good life and has made a better life for many people whom he never knew.

Thank you, June. God Bless.

There is another professional whom I would like to recognize as a true humanitarian. He's a resident of another city, Raleigh, NC, whom I've known for over thirty years. I haven't seen him for quite a few years, but we've had a few telephone conversations in the recent past. I have kept abreast of his activities through those calls and in other ways. We are very close to being the same age. I might have a year or two on him.

He has always struck me as being an affable person with a good humor. I've never seen him when he seemed unhappy. He struck me as being a person who enjoyed life and who looked forward to plying his profession as a psychiatrist every day. He met each day's challenge head on.

He served in the Korean War and achieved the rank of Major- and was awarded the bronze star. He was the second psychiatrist to establish a private practice in Raleigh and was widely known in his field of psychiatry.

In 1980 he was the only psychiatrist commissioned by Ciba-Geigy to handle the Anafranil protocol in North Carolina. In 1990 he was also commissioned to handle the second and last one for the same drug company. That one resulted in approval of the drug.

In 1994 Betts was forced to retire due to a broken leg and back trouble. He was eventually relegated to a wheel chair for ground transportation.

He was affected physically, but not mentally. He had no intention of stopping active life at that time. He wanted more of it in which he could find ways to help his fellow man. He wanted to make life better principally for those on a lower social level whom he did not know, however, he had been instrumental in the establishment of the NC Physicians Health Program for physicians dependent on drugs, prior to his retirement.

He has had a special interest in rehabilitating alcoholics. He had a large part in establishment of "The Healing Place" for homeless men-the detoxification unit being named "Betts Detoxcenter" in his honor. A few short years afterward, the private non-profit group with which he is associated also had a similar facility constructed for women and children.

Since his retirement he has been runner-up twice for the prestigious Kate B. Reynolds Award, which is presented annually to the North Carolinian who has contributed most to community service. He was bedridden for several weeks, but was back in his wheel chair last time I talked to him-he's the type of person the City of Raleigh, or any other city, can be proud of.

Yes-Dr. Wilmer Betts is another one of the professionals who has lived that good life and has passed it on to others.

*   *   *

I cannot leave this subject without paying homage to that enormous mass of ordinary human beings who make life better for others.

Due to the fact we are living longer lives, there are masses of people among us who cannot take care of themselves and are dependant on others for help. This help is coming more and more from within the family.

Spouses are taking care of each other. Parents are taking care of granddaddy and grandmamma. Grandparents are taking care of grandchildren. Friends are taking care of friends. What a wonderful gesture this has become. What would we do without these earthly angels who donate their time to the care and custody of others, giving them the chance of a better life?

I'm thinking of people with such names as Elizabeth, Mary Helen, Phil, Mary Ann, Plumer, Marvin, Christine, Tom, Leslie, Patricia, Martha, and Dean. The list could go on and on.

Then there are those who spontaneously respond to needs of others that surface on a spur of the moment, or short term basis. Like calling on the sick, taking a meal to the hungry, taking a cancer patient for treatment, delivering meals on wheels, or dozens of other little things over a period of weeks, months, or years. People who give their time freely, simply to make the small world of others a better place in which to live.

In that list I could put such names as Eleanor, Carolyn, Attie, Eddie, Tommy, and gobs of others. Yes, we really do have angels among us, and they make life better for others.

*   *   *

Ingredients

What are the ingredients that make up a good life? Where can we get them? Are they something we can simply reach out and grasp? Are they something we can buy? If so, what is the cost?

I don't know if anyone ever attempted to put a definition on the expression "good life", but my feeling is that it's principally made up of two feelings: happiness and contentment.

Let's tackle happiness first, since it's one of the rights given to us as Americans-"pursuit of happiness". It is something we can obtain in many ways.

Some people seem to achieve it by gaining financial wealth, after making it their goal in life. I knew a person years ago who, at age 25, made the statement that his goal was to be a millionaire by age 30. Actually, I believe he made it by age 29. I never knew if he secured real happiness when he reached that goal, or if he then set another goal of multiple millions.

I believe wealth really can make some people happy, but it does not dictate the extent to which happiness will reign in a household- and it does not guarantee peace of mind. If not properly managed, it can actually bring misery. At the same time, it's possible for an entire village of people living in poverty to be happy. And I don't believe it takes a village to rear a child.

A good environment, along with a good domestic situation, is also capable of bringing happiness to a family. A little leaguer who wins a ball game with a hit in the last inning can bask in the glory of happiness for a day. And what can be happier for a student than be told he passed his exams?

Yes, we can pursue happiness and sometimes catch up with it, but it can wax and wane. It can turn to sorrow so quickly. Peace of mind, however, can go a long way toward strengthening our grip on happiness.

That entity, however, is very elusive and is seldom obtained by most of us. If attained, it can make that good life we want much easier to secure. Even though that peace can't be purchased at any cost, it can be found in a number of ways on a short term basis.

Some are able to possess it by something as simple as a restful night's sleep. Others seem to secure it by successful completion of a seemingly insurmountable project. We can also have it on a longer lasting basis by asking forgiveness from others against whom we might have transgressed. Troubled minds hope to receive peace through prescription drugs, but the longest lasting peace seems to come through prayer, a meaningful relationship with God being the most important part of the person's life.

I believe peace of mind to be something that descends upon us like one of God's lovely, soft white clouds-enveloping us and bringing us unbelievable joy and contentment.

Attie Wiggins is one of those people endowed with the feeling of contentment. Barbara Rabhan is another, so is Billy Graham.

The other night our phone rang. I looked at the clock-9:00-a little late for us to be receiving phone calls. It was Mike calling from Asheville on Thursday night, a little unusual, especially since it had been only two days since he had called.

"Dad, Billy Graham is being interviewed by Larry King, if you're interested."

I had been watching the US Open being played at Pinehurst, NC, but I decided to switch channels, since I have followed the career of Reverend Graham for many years. I could catch up with the Open later.

I was intrigued by the answers this great white haired man of God was giving to King's questions-at age 87. King asked him if he were afraid of dying. His answer went something like this, "I welcome death at any time. For many years I have been ready to meet my God in paradise-it's something I've been looking forward to for years. About four years ago I thought I had finally reached the point when God would call me home. I had too much fluid on my brain and I was receiving a series of surgeries in an effort to alleviate the problem. I had a vision where I saw every sin I had ever committed passing before my eyes and I prayed to God to forgive me for every single one. At that time I felt a great sense of total peace envelop my whole body-and that peace is still in control of my body today."

"Do you have prostate cancer?" "Yes, I have prostate cancer." "Have you done anything about it?" "I take medication." "Do you have pain?" "No pain." "How is your wife's health?" "Not good-she's partially invalid."

"Would you like to die before she does?"

Hesitantly, "Well, what I would really like to do is join hands with Ruth and the both of us enter heaven together."

What a perfect example of contentment. Maybe peace of mind and contentment could come under the same definition: calmness, quietness, undisturbed state of mind, serenity or freedom from conflict within one's soul.

*   *   *

Unfortunately, there are some who never have the opportunity to achieve that good life feeling. Occasionally we read newspaper accounts of children being murdered by one parent or the other. Quite often the parents will say the devil made them do it, or that demons were involved.

Such an incident occurred about three or four years ago in Texas, in which a mother drowned all five of her children. Her explanation was that she had been surrounded by demons-and she was simply fulfilling a prophecy.

She believed the children would go to hell and be tormented if they were not killed. A psychiatrist testified that she was one of the sickest patients she had ever seen. The testimony had come as her lawyer made her case to the jury. She stated the defendant was innocent of a capital crime by reason of insanity, and that she should not be sentenced to death.

A doctor, who had interviewed the mother the day after the crime was committed, said the accused shouted to her, "I was so stupid! Couldn't I have killed just one to fulfill the prophecy? Couldn't I have just offered Mary?" Mary was the youngest child, only six months old.

During the examination, the mother had cried and pulled at her hair. She had then asked for her head to be shaved so she could point out a spot on her scalp where marks had been made by her continuous picking at it. She had referred to them as marks of the beast and 666. Five children never had the good life.

Trial lasted three weeks. Guilty of capital murder. Life sentence. Eligible for parole in 2041.

*   *   *

So, what makes life good for me, an 82 year old retired member of "The Greatest Generation"? Yes, I turned life's pages to eighty-two shortly ago-April 25, 2006.

Back in chapter nine I mentioned a number of major happenings that had made my life good. They were surely things of importance that enhanced my existence here on earth, but there are numerous small, sometimes inconspicuous, things that make for a good life for us old "geezers". (Did you know that word is defined as an eccentric old man?)

First of all, I love the idea of not having to get out of bed and go to work five days a week. I can remember those years when I slipped out of bed at 7 a.m., wishing I could have stayed there another hour.

Ironically, I now wake up at 6 a.m. and get up, because I can't go back to sleep. Oh, well. I'll offset that by taking a nap after supper.

I also like the flexibility of eating habits. Annie and I eat just whenever, regardless of the time of day. When I roll out of bed at six, I'm having breakfast at 6:15. Annie is still asleep and remains in that state until eight or nine, sometimes later than that. On Thursdays, however, she has to tumble off the mattress at 7:15 in order to meet her 8:00 hair appointment.

For lunch, most times we make do with a bowl of instant oatmeal- and maybe a Chewy. We usually prepare our evening meals for 5:00 consumption. That is, unless we decide to visit a nearby seafood buffet like the "Sandpiper" around 3:30. Most of our friends think we are weirdoes for eating our evening meal in the middle of the afternoon. Another thing that makes for a good life is senior prices at local restaurants.

Viewing beautiful aspects of nature can also enhance one's life. We have been fortunate enough to see some of the most beautiful floral gardens in our travels. I'm thinking of Butchart Gardens on Vancouver Island in British Columbia, the Elizabethan Gardens in the city of Vancouver, the School of Horticulture Floral Gardens at Niagara Falls, Canada, and Callaway Gardens in Georgia. All those places are beautiful, but we don't have to go that far away to enjoy nature's beauty. It's right here at my fingertips. Beautiful azaleas and dogwoods are beginning to bloom right now and it won't be long before crape myrtles will adorn our Kinston landscape.

But we don't have to wait for any of those to bloom. For the last two weeks we have had as pretty a sight right on our enclosed porch as I've seen anywhere.

Last Christmas Mike gave us an amaryllis bulb that is now in full bloom. It's a double (triple?) "red peacock"-fire red. Its stem is 23 inches tall and is adorned with five huge blossoms perfectly spaced around its tip. Each flower is about eight inches in diameter. The stem is perfectly straight, with no support. "A thing of beauty is a joy forever." And it helps make for a good life.

And how about having a three-year-old grandchild come up to you and say, "Granddaddy, will you please help me tie my shoe strings?" How about a six-year-old saying "thank you" while munching on a cone of chocolate? And having your ten-year-old saying, "Thank you Granddaddy", when you take his bike to the service station for air?

And it does your heart good when your fourteen-year-old writes you a note of thanks for his birthday card that had a greenback tucked inside big enough for a movie ticket and bucket of popcorn. And when he signs his name he always adds "I love you". Those are the little things that make our lives <u>really</u> good.

There are many hazards along life's journey that are unpleasant. Many battles to be fought. Many disappointments to incur-many ailments to endure. Yes, life is not a bed of roses, but in spite of all these negative factors I truly believe that for the vast majority of us, for the majority of the time, LIFE IS GOOD!

Numbers 6:24-26. "The Lord bless you and keep you; the Lord make his face shine upon you and be gracious to you; the Lord turn his face toward you and give you peace."

This is the author's second venture in writing. His first, <u>They Didn't Bring Ice On Sunday</u>, is the story of his life from birth to present. He chose to publish it in limited edition. In retrospect, it should have been published on a wider scale as it was very favorably received.

<u>Life is ...</u> is a roller coaster ride. It has peaks of exhilaration and valleys of despair. The author will make you happy and at times he will tug at your heartstrings. When he feels that the reader may be stretched a little, he will take you off the roller coaster. He will take you on a trip, tell you funny stories, and philosophize about life in general. He will quote scriptures to support his feelings about why things happen as they do. But rest assured, he will put you back on that roller coaster.

When I finished the manuscript and laid it down, I had a hard time letting it go. I started thinking about what life is to me. As I compared the author's ideas to my own, it occurred to me that is what the author intended. If it is, he accomplished his purpose.

Charles R. Brown

Printed in the United States
79601LV00003B/85-501